The Chartered Management Institute

chartered
management
institute

inspiring leaders

The Chartered Management Institute is the only chartered professional body that is dedicated to management and leadership. We are committed to raising the performance of business by championing management.

We represent 71,000 individual managers and have 450 corporate members. Within the Institute there are also a number of distinct specialisms, including the Institute of Business Consulting and Women in Management Network.

We exist to help managers tackle the management challenges they face on a daily basis by raising the standard of management in the UK. We are here to help individuals become better managers and companies develop better managers.

We do this through a wide range of products and services, from practical management checklists to tailored training and qualifications. We produce research on the latest 'hot' management issues, provide a vast array of useful information through our online management information centre, as well as offering consultancy services and career information.

You can access these resources 'off the shelf' or we can provide solutions just for you. Our range of products and services is designed to ensure companies and managers develop their potential and excel. Whether you are at the start of your career or a proven performer in the boardroom, we have something for you.

We engage policy makers and opinion formers and, as the leading authority on management, we are regularly consulted on a range of management issues. Through our in-depth research and regular policy surveys of members, we have a deep understanding of the latest management trends.

For more information visit our website **www.managers.org.uk** or call us on **01536 207307**.

Chartered Manager

Transform the way you work

The Chartered Management Institute's Chartered Manager award is the ultimate accolade for practising professional managers. Designed to transform the way you think about your work and how you add value to your organisation, it is based on demonstrating measurable impact.

This unique award proves your ability to make a real difference in the workplace.

Chartered Manager focuses on the six vital business skills of:

- Leading people
- Managing change
- Meeting customer needs
- Managing information and knowledge
- Managing activities and resources
- Managing yourself

Transform your organisation

There is a clear and well-established link between good management and improved organisational performance. Recognising this, the Chartered Manager scheme requires individuals to demonstrate how they are applying their leadership and change management skills to make significant impact within their organisation.

Transform your career

Whatever career stage a manager is at Chartered Manager will set them apart. Chartered Manager has proven to be a stimulus to career progression, either via recognition by their current employer or through the motivation to move on to more challenging roles with new employers.

instant manager
taking control of work and life

chartered
management
institute
inspiring leaders

dealing with
DIFFICULT
PEOPLE

KAREN MANNERING

HODDER
CATION
TE LIVRE UK

The publisher has used its best endeavours to ensure that the URLs for external websites referred to in this book are correct and active at the time of going to press. However, the publisher and the author have no responsibility for the websites and can make no guarantee that a site will remain live or that the content will remain relevant, decent or appropriate.

Orders: Please contact Bookpoint Ltd, 130 Milton Park, Abingdon, Oxon OX14 4SB. Telephone: (44) 01235 827720, Fax: (44) 01235 400454. Lines are open from 9.00 to 5.00, Monday to Saturday, with a 24-hour message answering service. You can also order through our website www.hoddereducation.co.uk.

British Library Cataloguing in Publication Data
A catalogue record for this title is available from the British Library.

ISBN-13: 978 0340 946 510

First published   2008
Impression number   10 9 8 7 6 5 4 3 2 1
Year   2012 2011 2010 2009 2008

Typeset by Transet Limited, Coventry, England.
Printed in Great Britain for Hodder Education, an Hachette Livre UK Company, 338 Euston Road, London NW1 3BH, by Cox & Wyman, Reading, Berkshire RG1 8EX.

Hachette Livre UK's policy is to use papers that are natural, renewable and recyclable products and made from wood grown in sustainable forests. The logging and manufacturing processes are expected to conform to the environmental regulations of the country of origin.

But don't take just our word for it ...

Chartered Manager has transformed the careers and organisations of managers in all sectors.

- *'Being a Chartered Manager was one of the main contributing factors which led to my recent promotion.'*
  Lloyd Ross, Programme Delivery Manager, British Nuclear Fuels

- *'I am quite sure that a part of the reason for my success in achieving my appointment was due to my Chartered Manager award which provided excellent, independent evidence that I was a high quality manager.'*
  Donaree Marshall, Head of Programme Management Office, Water Service, Belfast

- *'The whole process has been very positive, giving me confidence in my strengths as a manager but also helping me to identify the areas of my skills that I want to develop. I am delighted and proud to have the accolade of Chartered Manager.'*
  Allen Hudson, School Support Services Manager, Dudley Metropolitan County Council

- *'As we are in a time of profound change, I believe that I have, as a result of my change management skills, been able to provide leadership to my staff. Indeed, I took over three teams and carefully built an integrated team, which is beginning to perform really well. I believe that the process I went through to gain Chartered Manager status assisted me in achieving this and consequently was of considerable benefit to my organisation.'*
  George Smart, SPO and D/Head of Resettlement, HM Prison Swaleside

To find out more or to request further information please visit our website **www.managers.org.uk/cmgr** or call us on **01536 207429**.

Contents

CHAPTER 03

DIFFICULT EMPLOYEES – HOW DO I DEAL WITH THEM

CHAPTER 04

DIFFICULT MANAGERS – HOW DO I DEAL WITH THEM?

CHAPTER 05

DIFFICULT COLLEAGUES – HOW DO I DEAL WITH THEM?

CHAPTER 06

DIFFICULT CUSTOMERS – HOW DO I DEAL WITH THEM?

CHAPTER 07

DIFFICULT SUPPLIERS – HOW SHOULD I DEAL WITH THEM?   107

CHAPTER 08

HOW DO I DEAL WITH DIFFICULT PEOPLE FROM OTHER CULTURES AND COUNTRIES   123

CHAPTER 09

HOW DO I COPE IF I AM THE ONE BEING DIFFICULT?

CHAPTER 10

HOW CAN I MANAGE CONFLICTING TEAM MEMBERS

Preface

Welcome to *Dealing with Difficult People*. You may have had several reasons for buying this book. Perhaps you are moving into a supervisory or management role and wish to prepare, or maybe you already have a number of difficult people crowding your life. Whatever the situation, this book provides an overview of how to deal with difficult people and offers practical advice divided into specific sections. Exercises and case studies help you put the advice into perspective and towards the back of the book you will find not only suggested solutions but also a Twelve-Point Tool Box of tips and techniques that cross all situations.

So, here we go.

01

What do we mean by a difficult person?

Who are the difficult people in your life? How do you decide that they are 'difficult'? Is it an instant feeling you get about someone or the result of a degenerating relationship? Is it about personalities or business?

However you answered the above questions most of us have people in our life who we consider difficult, and when this situation is at work, we cannot simply walk away. You can choose your friends but not your work colleagues and when difficult people are in your team, you simply have to find a way forward. People are the most important resource in any organisation, and the ability to communicate at a high level is critical for career success. Individuals deemed to have high levels of emotional intelligence are able to adapt their communication style to manage all types of people, especially the difficult ones. Therefore communicating effectively with challenging characters demonstrates specific skills that not everyone possesses. The good news is that these skills are not necessarily innate and can be learnt, so let's start learning.

The *Oxford English Dictionary* defines 'difficult' as being:

'troublesome, perplexing, unaccommodating, stubborn'

… and indeed these are some of the types of people we will be discussing, together with those who are aggressive, selfish, negative, overly accommodating, insecure and high maintenance.

However, before we look at individual traits we need to establish some facts.

The 'One Universal Truth'

There is one universal truth that we need to accept before we can proceed:

There is no quick fix or magic wand that changes the behaviour of others.

You may have seen 'mind benders' and hypnotists on the stage and television, but as a qualified clinical hypno-psychotherapist I can tell you that there are no quick fixes to instant behavioural change, and any behavioural modification must be desired by the person concerned. In short, they will have found good reasons for displaying the type of behaviour they exhibit – it works for them and they get what they want. We need to show them that there is another way that not only also works, but is even more effective.

This means that behavioural change cannot be forced. We have all experienced wanting to be liked by someone, perhaps at school, and the other person not responding in the way we want. It is a hard lesson in life that we cannot make others like us, want us, or even love us – we can only model positive behaviour, influence and encourage, and hope that the other person feels the same. This is, in fact, excellent news. It means that whenever we notice behavioural change in others it is because they want to adapt or rethink the way they interact with us, and try a different approach. They are meeting us halfway, playing by the rules, and this makes for pleasant interaction.

So if we cannot change everyone to our preferred way of behaving, where does that leave us? Well, the only thing that we can effectively change is ourselves – our own behaviour. This means having a number of techniques to hand and being open to try flexible approaches in applying them.

For example, John has just started working in your team. You have noticed that he works incessantly. He never takes a break, even through lunchtime, and that is frowned on by your organisation as they put great store on work/life balance and the need to take regular breaks. There is a real danger that if John continues, and then has a breakdown, you (as his manager) may be held responsible. Now you could tackle this in two ways:

1. You could call John in and lay the law down, telling him that this is not how you work here. It is affecting the rest of the team and they are starting to feel resentful, and therefore you will need to monitor him more closely. Or:

2. You could call John in, and engage him in more gentle conversation, trying in the first instance to find out whether he feels confident about his job or has any worries. Then, without sounding accusational, you could mention how the organisation views overwork and drop into the conversation how you find breaks so refreshing and that perhaps John should join you on one, or go with a colleague. (You may want to inject an analogy or a story to illustrate your point.) Then make sure that John sees you taking regular breaks yourself.

You may be thinking that the first way is so much quicker and less hassle but the outcome will be very different. With the first way, John will feel shamed, caught out; he will know that his colleagues have been speaking about him and that now he has done 'something wrong' he needs to be monitored. This will make John feel bad, and is not a good start to your relationship. The second way may take a little longer but demonstrates your real skill as a manager. You are hoping that John changes his behaviour because *he decides to* and therefore retains his self-esteem and confidence. He will see you as a leader rather than a bully and he will appreciate the care of your guidance. He does not feel ashamed or that he has done anything wrong, and is quite happy to go back to the team, knowing that your conversation stays between the two of you. The fact that you are modelling this behaviour yourself shows John that it is acceptable to work in this way and that it is, in fact, expected. This all bodes well for John working in your team for a long time.

At this point you might be thinking that you picked up this book to change other people, not to have to change yourself. After all the problem is 'out there' isn't it? Not in here with you. Behaviour is a type of communicational dance, as we will see below, and the quality of the dance depends heavily on both partners.

Your role in the dynamic

Almost every time I am involved in mediation or some kind of dispute, I am called upon to change the behaviour of the other person because they are being difficult. It is so easy to think that every problem is because of the other person's 'difficult' personality, but in every interaction we cannot separate ourselves (or anyone else involved) from the dynamic.

What do I mean? Imagine you are walking down a corridor near to your office and you see two colleagues having a conversation about a third person. They are speaking and gesturing in ways they can both understand. As you pass you hear something of interest and decide to join the conversation. Suddenly the conversational rules need to change to accommodate you being present.

Your colleagues may use different phrases or examples to illustrate their conversation, and if you are in any way related to or a friend of any of the characters being discussed, they will be very careful as to how they express their opinions. The point here is that you have had an impact on the way the communication can continue, that cannot be ignored. The conversational 'dance' has changed to accommodate a third 'dancer' and therefore the rules of the dance need to change.

When dealing with people in a difficult scenario we have to accept ourselves as being part of the situation. Power, status, personality and a whole host of other issues have an impact on the situation, and ultimately the outcome. It may be hard for each of us to consider that we may be part of the problem – but in simply accepting that this may be so, and watching for any of the signs, we could be part-way to finding a solution (we will discuss this more in Chapter 9).

The fact that we are part of the dynamic in any interaction means that we need to consider our own behaviour (verbal and non-verbal) at all times. We need to take full responsibility for the things we say and do to make sure we are part of the solution rather than a continuation of the problem.

Different types of difficult behaviour

To describe someone as 'difficult' is all encompassing. However, the degree or nature of the difficulty can vary from person to person. Let's look at a number of typically difficult behaviours here and see where these people may be coming from, as sometimes an insight into their behaviour can help us understand them, and therefore consequently deal with them, better.

Remember that popular psychology tells us that we must have some kind of reward for perpetuating our behaviour, and therefore an insight to where the motivation may come from is useful.

Aggressive people

You may be very well aware of aggressive people already – they stand tall, make a lot of noise and generally try to frighten and intimidate those about them. Of all the difficult types of people, aggressives make their presence widely known and are possibly the most openly feared of all the types.

In essence this is not true. Yes, they can make a big noise, which makes them scary, but they are the WYSIWYGs of the business world. In other words, what you see is what you get. This obvious 'front' to their behaviour makes them easier to handle than some of their more devious counterparts. If you can get past the noise, then you might find out what is going on.

What motivates them? Well, clearly this behaviour has worked well for them in the past. They come from the school of 'shout loud enough and others will hear, and push hard enough and others will have to take notice.' Some aggressives even relish this side of their personas, recommending that it is the only way to get things done, and even go so far as modelling themselves on currently fashionable aggressive personalities. It is likely that somewhere in their past they have struggled to be heard. Perhaps they were a middle child or ignored to some extent. They have learnt that the only way to push through their ideas is to become aggressive (and that often means loud). As this behaviour scares so many people, it works, and as they cave in to the aggressive's bullying tactics, this acceptance reinforces the aggressive further. This behaviour has to be right – it delivers results, doesn't it?

Aggressives need a firm stance. You have to stand up to them and be clear about how their behaviour affects you and the others around you. Many aggressives appear to be astounded when told that their behaviour strikes fear into others; they feel they are being nothing more than vocally assertive. This mismatch in perceptions needs to be explored in some detail before change can begin to take place.

Harassment laws are in place to prevent bullying in the workplace, and managers need to discuss this openly with all staff. So where is the incentive to change? Aggressives need to be:

- faced with their behaviour
- informed of the problems this causes (giving instances)
- notified of the consequences
- given an alternative route for behaviour.

Note: Not all aggressives would become violent but should it be threatened, this is one area where you immediately need to involve other authorities such as the police.

Know-it-alls

The main aspect of the know-it-all appears to be their irritating obsession with knowing everything, but slightly more worrying is their inability to listen. These are not the specialists known in every business, they are the busy bodies whom you find it difficult to stop once they are on a roll. Their knowledge may not even be that special or interesting but if they hear a question in your voice, they will be straight in there. Know-it-alls jump in before you have even finished your sentence, such is their keenness to demonstrate that they truly do know it all, and to state their claim to this knowledge before anyone else speaks. This means that, while they are gabbling, they are not listening to the tail end of your message. That could be a real problem, especially if you have designed a particularly punchy ending or have left the most significant facts until last.

Below the surface of the know-it-all is the child who needs to feel important. They are searching for recognition that comes with information. Knowledge is power, and they know how to use it. Know-it-alls hope to dazzle with facts and are craving attention and approval through their behaviour. It may be that they are slightly weak in other areas of business, but are able to dominate in this one area. Every manager needs expertise and information, but it is the manner in which this is given that makes for smooth communication.

This brings me to the final point. The know-it-all usually has a certain, even if understated, arrogance. When they give information it is delivered in such a way as to elevate themselves and put down others. The information then becomes game points that result in the know-it-all being the winner, superior in some way over the other players, who may not even have understood that they were in a game.

Know-it-alls need lots of reassurance; they need to feel important. Ways to deal with this could include:

- harnessing some of their enthusiasm by praising their knowledge
- balancing that out by praising others at the same time too
- being assertive in stopping them interrupting or cutting across you by asking them to allow you to finish each section of what you are trying to say
- giving feedback on their behaviour and how it affects you.

Note: Know-it-alls can be quite thick-skinned and therefore you may have to do this many times before they get the message.

Selfish people

Selfish people don't share and that means anything from a pencil sharpener to a business idea. There may be a number of reasons for this – perhaps they had trouble sharing as children, perhaps they have never had to, and so now are unsure how. This may not be an issue for them in their private lives. However, when we are considering a work situation, items at work often have status values, and whether we share them or not gives an insight as to how comfortable we are about our own individuality. Staff can become very protective of the chair they sit in, which workstation they use, and whether they have to share an office or not. Another layer of complexity is that some items in the workplace may be privately owned (such as staff bringing in their own pen or calendar) whilst other items may be under the ownership of the company. This differential matters to some staff, for example they may be happy to share something that clearly belongs to the company, such as a computer, but not anything that belongs to them personally, like a pack of specialist erasers.

Selfish people may not share ideas either. They lack team spirit and cannot always see the benefit in giving away something that may have currency for them later on. This does not mean they are not good workers; they may work very well in specialist roles or in isolation, but their input still needs to be managed.

When dealing with selfish staff, it might be helpful first to work out, what you are asking them to share. Is it just a computer workstation or do these items have status currency in your workplace? What does sharing this item or information mean to them personally? Is it about the item or is there a deeper concern, perhaps around the individual's identity or level of power? If so, the issue might be bigger than just sharing equipment. You might be asking them to share status or boundaries, which are far more emotive. Getting them to talk about themselves and look behind the issue may be quite revealing and open up a whole area of conversation. Many people today are curious about why they think the way they do, and psychology books abound. Chat to them about what they think provides status – the place they sit, their desk, computers, personal space, information? At one place I worked, only senior staff were allowed time management systems, and at another (believe it or not) it was desklamps. They came to mean more than the object, and people became very ownership-orientated. Careful questioning may offer useful insight for the individual, and at the same time will give the message that this behaviour is not viewed favourably, at least within the business setting.

In the first instance:

- identify what exactly they are being selfish about (ideas, items, furniture)
- speak to them about how they see their identity in the team
- challenge them with their behaviour and try to find out what they think they will lose by sharing
- encourage them by bolstering their own ego and place in the team
- give them more joint projects where they have to work with someone else to achieve a successful outcome.

Negative people

Everyone knows someone who is negative but before you label them a complete 'nay sayer', consider that it may be a defence mechanism to prevent them from being rejected, shocked or hurt. Nevertheless, their behaviour can rankle and their effect can be widespread.

Negative people bring not only you but also the whole team down. Their glass is always half empty and they take pleasure in providing everyone with the 'worst case' scenarios at every opportunity. Rather than viewing their comments as negative, they often reason that they are merely being more realistic about events. They cannot understand why others are so over-optimistic, change can never be good, can it? Something always has to go wrong, doesn't it?

One of the main problems with negative people is that they don't realise how damaging their comments are to the other people around them. Everyone is entitled to their own opinion, but when it affects others in the team, or work colleagues, you may have to step in. Never argue with negative people, instead try to agree with them but take the conversation on a step further. If they say to you, 'We tried that before and it did not work then so it will not work now,' answer by saying, 'You may be proved right but things have changed around here and I want to give the idea another go.' Negative people will never inspire, enthuse, or generally motivate – in short they will not make good leaders. However, all organisations need, 'Ah, but' people, and they have a valuable role to play in monitoring ideas before the 'positives' become too carried away by their own brilliant suggestions.

It would be almost impossible to change a fully negative person into a positive one so you are trying to make slight changes:

- Don't put them down. Instead acknowledge their views and then offer a counter approach, for example, 'Yes, this may fail, but I'm going to give it my best shot anyway.'
- Try to phrase suggestions in a positive format for them, such as, 'I'm sure you won't mind helping out on this task.'
- Acknowledge their role in the team: 'We need someone to be devil's advocate here, just to make sure we are on the right road. What about you, Mary? Challenge these ideas and let's see if they stand up to scrutiny.'
- If their negativity has a profound effect on the group, you may need to speak to them on a one-to-one basis but make sure the conversation sticks to their comments and behaviours and is not personal.

Passive people and passive-aggressives

Passive people do not join in activities; they prefer to sit on the sidelines. They may not enter into team discussions, preferring to say nothing in the belief that if they say nothing they will not be wrong. They are often passive in all parts of their life, believing that great things happen only to other people, and that everyone else has far more power to make changes than they have. The problem here is that they do their job with little enthusiasm, never volunteer for tasks and appear to have a sense of moving through life rather than taking part in it. They are not particularly frightening (in fact you are more likely to frighten them) but again they can bring the team down.

Passivity is often linked to low self-esteem and therefore passive people need to:

- have their role acknowledged in the team
- be given specific pieces of work to undertake, bring back and discuss (to encourage them to engage)
- have positive feedback from everyone
- be encouraged to take an active part in meetings.

Their far more sinister partners are the passive-aggressives. They are the ones who say nothing in the meeting but mutter aggressive comments under their breath. In a sense they are cowards, hiding their comments behind their hand or papers. They can do a lot of damage in a team because they appear demure during the meeting but then out comes the poison later. If caught they often refer to childish behaviour, 'What me? I never said anything!'

In common with so many other different types of difficult people, passive-aggressives may not acknowledge their traits. They may feel that they present a timid, shy or scared person who is often the victim of situations and other people.

The Achilles heel of passive-aggressives is that they hate to be found out or exposed. They are happy to spread their poison but it has to be in secret. They are the snipers behind the throne, and they lash out with intent to do real harm. They harm you as a manager because they cut across all your intended actions and belittle them to the other staff, and they harm the others in the team because their sniping is very destructive and destabilising. It is not long before they hold an overly influential role in the team, and that can be very wearing for everyone. Many passive-aggressives are bullies or go on to become them.

When dealing with passive-aggressives you need to:

- have hard evidence of what they said and when they said it (this can be more tricky than you think because they cover their tracks well)
- confront them with their comments, and ask them for the reasons behind their behaviour
- explain the way in which their bad behaviour affects the team (including team morale)
- ask them in future to speak up with their comments within the meeting, so that you have a chance to discuss all matters at the time and they can be minuted if appropriate.

Passive-aggressives are not easy to stop, as their behaviour may have become ingrained. However, it is not to be tolerated. Refer them to any policies you may have on misconduct and start keeping notes.

Overly accommodating people

These people can be difficult in that they desperately want to please. They often have low self-esteem and can be annoyingly attentive in their need to be of use to someone else. It is not difficult to place these people under extreme pressure and overwork them because they say nothing until they become resentful or collapse. If you ask them to do a task they often rush off to do it immediately and leave their other work (which may not have been the best way to do it or the most efficient use of time). They are desperately seeking approval and may become depressed if they don't get the thanks they feel they deserve. In a sense they are like a dog wanting a stick to be thrown and expecting a pat in return for its retrieval.

Overly accommodating people mean to be helpful but that can manifest itself as being clingy and irksome. With their own lack of self-confidence they put other people on a pedestal, which although may appear wonderful to start with, becomes irritating after a period of time. (Also, being up on a pedestal means that you have a very long way to fall into disgrace, if and when that happens.) Pushing them away seems to either enhance their need to get closer, or upset them terribly, so what can you do?

Overly accommodating people need:

- to be valued – their self-esteem needs a big lift so work on building their inner confidence rather than offering platitudes
- to know about boundaries – set some times when they cannot gain access to you. This will help you to get some work done and relieve them of the pressure of having to dance to your tune. Have a code such as putting up a sign for when you must not be interrupted
- to be given time management and assertiveness training – this will enable them to set their priorities for the day and help stick to them
- a significant project of their own to work on so that they achieve a solid outcome
- regular workplace monitoring to ensure they do not overwork.

Insecure people

Insecurity can manifest itself in a number of ways. On the one hand the insecure member of staff may be quiet and hang back from the rest of the team, or conversely they may compensate by being overly aggressive. Behaviourally speaking, an insecure animal will shake, shiver and may bite. While you do not expect that of staff, the underlying feelings may be very similar.

The important thing here is to identify, if possible, the insecurity. If you are able to do that, you can begin to work with whatever you find. For example, if you discover that a member of staff is insecure because they have a lower level of numeracy than they admitted to on their application form, you can take action in a number of ways. Similarly, if it is revealed that their insecurity emanates from a bullying member of the team, again appropriate action can be taken. It is therefore crucial to try to identify and eliminate the reason for the insecurity. (If you suspect the cause to be something that lies outside of the workplace, there are a number of support systems you could advise such as contacting therapists, psychotherapists, clinical hypnotists, counsellors and so forth to enable your staff member to get the best help. Many organisations now offer counselling or support through third parties as part of the employment package.)

Insecure people need:

- appropriate questioning to find out where their insecurities lie
- lots of support, both physically and psychologically
- ongoing confidence building and esteem strengthening
- high quality feedback.

High maintenance people

High maintenance people are just that, they take up all your time. This may be because they are demanding attention or just very needy. High maintenance behaviour comes from a number or sources. They could have been an only child, used to a continuous audience, or perhaps they were born into a large family where only the one who shouts the loudest gets heard. If they are fairly young, they may even not know that this type of behaviour is not relevant in a work setting.

Behind the high maintenance person could lie a deep insecurity of either their position within the team, or their work. Notice how their activity is focused – is it on the work (they have to ask you to make every decision for them or check over every detail) or is it more about posturing and aligning themselves with you. If the person is senior to yourself it may be that they feel the need to assert their status by being demanding. If this is the case you need to work out how much attention and contact you believe is reasonable, discuss this with them, and then see if you can create a workable environment. After all, if you are being paid to be a valet then you could expect your employer to want you to be near them most of the time – after all they are the focus of your job. However, if you work in an office environment the focus is different and you will need to manage your own workload too.

Whatever the reason you desperately need to get your life back. While you are dealing with high maintenance people you are not concentrating on your job, and getting your own work done. High maintenance people will have you running in circles around them, and you just don't have the time.

High maintenance people need:

- clear boundaries – they need to know when they can and cannot approach you. Consider setting some times of the day when you are not to be disturbed

- to know that they are doing their job properly – give them lots of good quality feedback and written notes in one-to-one sessions
- to be faced with their behaviour and told that it is untenable – but be given an opportunity to explain and start afresh
- to perhaps have a secret signal or sign that you can do to indicate that they have had enough of your time. It will allow them to withdraw with their self-esteem intact.

INSTANT TIP

Each one of us has the potential to be difficult. Remember that we all come to a situation from a different perspective, and any confrontation takes two people.

02

Is there any way that I can read people?

Wouldn't it be great to be able to read what people are thinking? If it were possible, then perhaps we could head off any of the difficulties in their behaviour. Well, the good news is that the information is present if we know where to look for it, and if we take the effort to look for it. Yes, that's right, it takes real effort on our part because we are not necessarily used to using the intuitive side of our nature on a daily basis.

How have we lost the use of this very useful part of our nature? Essentially we are all animals and as animals we have retained our primitive ways of communication. We sense moods and attitudes in others in the same way that our pets can in us. Have you ever been in the situation whereby you know something is wrong with another person, but you just cannot put your finger on what it is or how exactly you know? That is your behavioural intuition at work. Thousands of years ago it was all we had, but because we have developed such a sophisticated system of verbal communication today, we tend to ignore these signals and rely totally on what we hear. In doing this we are missing out on a whole range of signals that are being sent, some of which we may not even be aware of.

To ignore these would be foolish and so we need to tap into this forgotten source of data once again and regain the lost art of reading people.

Our internal filters

Once information comes to us it needs to be processed. For this we use the internal filters that are unique to each of us. These filters put information – verbal, nonverbal and intuitive signals – into context. The fact that our filters are unique accounts for the varying meaning we put on interpretation. For example, both you and I may be having a conversation with Jim about the fact that he is behind with his project. Jim is keen to reassure us both that he is now up to date with his work. Jim is exhibiting the same verbal and nonverbal signals to both of us, but I may read his comments in a different way to you. You may be reassured that the project is back on line, while I may think that Jim demonstrated that he is hiding something. Who is right? Well in a way we both are because we have seen Jim's response through our own personal filters. My filters tell me that in the past when I have seen Jim (or even someone else) exhibiting those 'tells' they indicate a cover-up of some kind. Your filters, based on your experience, either tell you that Jim is telling the truth, or perhaps you are choosing not to see messages that you don't want to see.

These filters come from our experiences through life. The more we see and deal with people, the greater the bank of filters that build up. This is a great thought to have when you are placed in any difficult situation – you may be feeling discomfort at that particular time but you are actually adding and refining more experiences to add to your own personal data bank.

How does this data bank (called your brain) work? It works by making links. Let me ask you a question. How do you recognise that the animal coming towards you is a dog? You have an imprinted prototype of a dog in your brain. When you see something that looks like a dog – four legs, one head, covered in hair – whether it is a Chihuahua or a Great Dane, you will recognise it as being a dog. Even more amazing is the fact that you will not think a lion is a dog even though they share many of the same physical characteristics. These amazing filters work for us in all manner of ways, including how we communicate with other human beings. Our ability to differentiate between similar faces and expressions is incredible. Aristotle said that 'In order to learn to play the flute you have to play the flute'. In other words, when you are learning you have to practise and get stuck into real experiences. Therefore you need to experience as many difficult situations as you can in life and then you will have a rich data bank of knowledge to draw on when you need to know whether the object in front of you is a terrier or a panther.

Visual 'tells'

Do faces and bodies give away signals? Can we tell whether someone is going to be an awkward customer just by looking at them? Certainly some people look more disagreeable than others, but is that always a reliable indication of their mood? I'm sure you will have experienced meeting someone who you initially thought to be cantankerous, only to find them charming when you got to know them. Therefore you cannot always make sweeping assumptions about someone from a downturned mouth, a furrowed brow or thin lips. Always be cautious about jumping to conclusions with such unqualified 'information'.

So what can you do? The face provides information in two ways. Firstly, by physical attributes, such as thin lips or thick eyebrows, as mentioned above. These can make us think that people look mean or angry when this probably isn't true. Secondly, the face gives us information by expressions or facial actions. We have a very limited degree of control over the former, but greater control over the latter. For example, we can force a smile whether we are feeling happy or not. In fact, we have such control over our faces that, when required, many of us could choose to present any facial expression most convincingly. If it were not so, actors would not be able to portray realistic emotions on screen, and have us believe in them.

Facially speaking

The study of body language comes from a mixture of:

- anthropology (the study of animal behaviour)
- neuro-linguistic programming (the study of the interconnectivity between the brain and our language), and
- social psychology (where the social setting and people involved may affect the behaviour).

It is no exact science but certain theories have shown to be most reliable. Experiments into facial recognition have identified five major facial 'tells' that are common all over the world. They are:

- sadness
- fear
- happiness
- disgust
- anger.

The miraculous thing about this is that it is an innate quality that appears to cross cultures and boundaries, even in those cultures who have less expressive faces themselves. Therefore you most certainly *will* recognise these emotions when you see them, giving you pre-preparation time to greet the person in the most

IS THERE ANY WAY THAT I CAN READ PEOPLE?

appropriate manner. For example, if you see someone coming towards you displaying an angry facial configuration, consider that they are just that – angry – and greet them with concern for their problem, rather than ignoring such basic facial tells and greeting them with a sunny smile.

The face is a very important part of the body as it is the showcase for many of our emotions. Mothers often stroke around the face area of a baby when they are feeding and the gesture is very comforting (just think of the popularity of facial massages). Because of this, self-touching of the facial area is often an indication of inner discomfort, anxiety or lack of confidence in the protagonist. If someone is feeling in a stressful situation, they need to gain some fast comfort for their woes. Facial touching, whether that be stroking around the chin area, up the side of the face, pushing hair back from the face, or even playing with earrings, provides a 'soft stroking' or self-comfort gesture. This indicates to you as observer that the person is experiencing anxiety. Depending on the situation you, as a manager, may wish to lessen their anxiety and attempt to make them feel more comfortable by using softer, encouraging words and gestures. However, this information is also useful in a conflict situation or when speaking to someone directly about their negative behaviour. It would indicate that the person exhibiting these gestures may not be as cool and composed with you as they are trying to appear. They may be feeling out of their comfort zone or anxious about the discussion you are both having. When we are in a difficult conflict situation with another person it can easily seem like they have the upper hand, and if we are fearful of what they may say, there is the possibility of becoming defensive, which helps no one. Seeing these gestures as anxiety tells and knowing that the other person is finding the interaction difficult, can change the nature of the conversation, and consequently the outcome. We react very differently to people when we know they are finding the conversation difficult: we may even be quite supportive. No matter what is being said, pay attention to these gestures, and you may find that you can gain the upper hand in many conflict situations.

There are also a number of facial 'tells' that, although not proven conclusively, are common across a wide proportion of people. For example, when many people think or ponder on a response, their eyes go slightly up to their left. It can vary from a slight movement to a strong and lengthy one. This is thought to be the case because to consider all aspects of an issue or question, people need to access the left side of their brain, which takes on a more logical function, storing large amounts of data in streams and connections that need to be searched. (Although the brain is very interconnected, the right side is thought to deal mainly with more abstract, immediate and creative data.) Ask your colleagues a question that requires them to think hard to answer (perhaps about something that may have happened in their childhood) and see whether this is true of them. It may only be a tiny movement, but look for that quick flick of the pupil before the eyes return to focus on you. If you find that this is correct for your particular work colleagues you will always be able to see whether they are really considering your new proposal fully – or just saying they are. Neuro linguistic programming (NLP) is the study of brain-to-verbal communication. It also incorporates body language nuances, and that includes eye movement. NLP studies teach us that different parts of the brain are responsible for handling different aspects of thought processes, and that the eyes move to indicate whatever thought process is being used. A typical eye movement sequence is shown in Figure 2.1 and again it can help to give us information about other people. In the diagram you will see that the eyes move to different parts of the socket when accessing different types of information. For example, if you ask someone to relay a conversation that they heard earlier, their eyes (if they are right-handed), should move to their left as they do so. If their eyes moved up to their right, it is more likely that they are constructing images

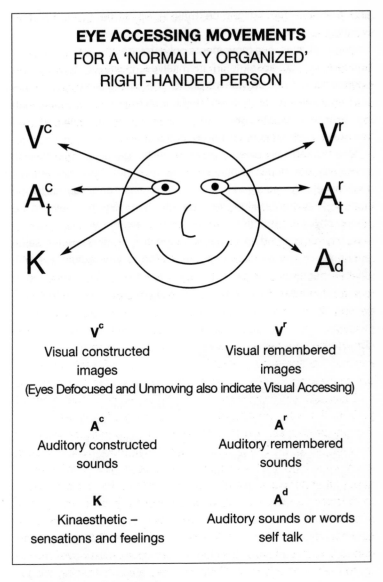

EYE ACCESSING MOVEMENTS
FOR A 'NORMALLY ORGANIZED'
RIGHT-HANDED PERSON

V^c

Visual constructed
images

V^r

Visual remembered
images

(Eyes Defocused and Unmoving also indicate Visual Accessing)

A^c

Auditory constructed
sounds

A^r

Auditory remembered
sounds

K

Kinaesthetic –
sensations and feelings

A^d

Auditory sounds or words
self talk

Figure 2.1: Eye accessing movements

and therefore they might be making up some story, possibly creating a meeting that did not really happen. Like all body language studies, eye movements only provide the flavour of insight and are not an absolute in themselves. However, they remain interesting and can provide insight. Start noticing body movements such as eye movements as they will tell you more about people than you ever thought possible. In other words, you are learning to read their tells rather than relying on words alone.

Many people are aware that when we are genuinely interested in someone, our pupils dilate. This research has been undertaken extensively, especially in dating situations, and found to be amazingly accurate. However, the situation does not have to be about physical attraction. Gazing at a desirable watch, piece of jewellery, or just finding someone interesting would have the same effect. Again you can use this information to your advantage with difficult people. Look into their eyes. Are they really interested in you, your ideas and presentations or just paying lip service to them?

Body giveaways

The face is not the only information hot spot. Bodies generate volumes of information. The way we stand, move, twist and turn and, of course, our arm gestures, tell anyone willing to notice just what we really think. For example, when we like someone we move in rapport with them. Moving in rapport simply means that we use similar gestures and positioning of the body, which communicates as 'you are just like me'.

Exercise

Look at people who either get on very well or who regularly work together. This can be done in work time or even over lunch. See how rapport affects their body movements. It could be that they sit with their legs crossed and lean towards each other when talking, or perhaps they start using very similar arm gestures. Now think about the last time you were in a situation with someone difficult. I doubt very much that you moved in rapport with them. What about when you are unsure? If you are not receiving these messages and the other person's body language is not in rapport with yours, and does not appear to be moving towards it, beware. It could be that they do not want to align themselves with you – or any of your ideas.

Much has been written concerning body language and the meanings attributed to certain gestures, some of it helpful and some of it less so. It is very difficult to generalise in many cases as, being very sophisticated and complex animals, we even create our own 'designer' body tells that work only for us. However, there are some anthropological generalisations that underpin most of these unique tells, and understanding these can help to reveal some of our deepest insecurities.

Most people would agree that the trunk of the human body contains the valuable organs without which we would fail to function, and of the trunk, the chest is the most vulnerable part. It is not surprising then that when we feel vulnerable we feel the need to protect this area. This can be exhibited in many different ways. Firstly, the shoulders can come very slightly forward producing a round-shouldered look. This can be made up of minute tightening movements as the chest area attempts to make itself a smaller surface area. Sometimes this is enough, but on occasions when the discomfort is more acute, a second barrier may be introduced.

This is often in the form of an arm either in a direct movement (possibly diagonally across the chest ending with a hand on the opposite shoulder or in a 'Y' shape to the throat), or a less direct movement (such as the unnecessary tightening of a tie at the knot, or playing with a necklace). These movements are often involuntary and the other person will not even be aware of doing them.

Exercise

Do another spot of people watching and see how others react when they feel 'exposed' to something they find threatening. This could be a reaction to another person, or to more challenging work. Also become aware of your own tells in this area. When you feel vulnerable or insecure, how do you 'protect' your own chest area? What is this saying to other people?

Another area where our body language can give us away is in the upper torso. A large number of people carry tension in their neck muscles. This means that when someone feels tense or under pressure, their shoulders are raised a little higher than normal, and the whole upper torso becomes stiff and less flexible. This can result in the person having a more solid but 'wooden' look that is perceptible to others. Similarly, if someone is coming towards you in an aggressive manner, they often pull themselves up to their full height and make their upper body as wide as possible. It is the human equivalent of having your feathers or fur stand on end. One thing that is helpful to know when dealing with someone demonstrating this body position (through whatever circumstance) is that maintaining it is incredibly energy consuming. In fact no one can maintain this state indefinitely, and when they do 'come down' they will be physically depleted. Their energy is sapped, they are tired, and in extreme circumstances they may even cry. When this happens, do not use their depleted energy as an excuse to counterattack. Instead try to give out 'I am listening to you' tells such as nodding and acknowledging their comments in a quiet, controlled manner until they are ready to speak with you calmly. Although they cannot stay in this high state of anger indefinitely, they need to deal with handling the resulting loss of energy in a dignified way. Interrupting, trying to speak over them, or appearing falsely sympathetic will either increase their anger further to explosion point or induce them to walk out, neither of which will solve the situation.

Hands and arms are another body tell. Look at the person you are speaking to. Are their hands giving wide expansive gestures or are they tightly in a ball? Are they relaxed to the sides or gesturing wildly and indicating some form of excitement? Look where they are in relation to the rest of the body and at the tension in the fingers. The person in front of you may not be shouting but if their hands are tightly clenched and their knuckles are white, they may be near to boiling point.

We have already mentioned some positioning of the hands and arms. If placed in proximity to the face and neck, the look is defensive. Aggressive hands make firm slicing and fist thumping movements. This is also something you can borrow if you want to add more dynamism to a speech or appear more decisive. Hands clasped behind the back always look somewhat unnatural because we don't naturally stand that way. This stance can make the person appear strict and upright, like a teacher, or childlike, depending on the rest of the body movements. Over-expressive arms presented with the right level of enthusiasm can be flamboyant and can give the impression of power and positivity. Once again the audience feels like you are literally filling the room with your presence. (Lacking the crucial element of passion could, however, see you looking more like a windmill or helicopter!)

Lies, damned lies and statistics

The thing that we all want to know is whether there are any certain 'tells' that expose liars. Scratching that itch around the nose area and in fact any movement of the hands around the nose and mouth area tend to be interpreted as lying 'tells' but be careful – the other person may just have an itchy nose!

If there are any sure signs, all I can say is that the police and the courts would find them most interesting! Hands around and covering the mouth, rubbing of the back of the neck, or a failure to make eye contact may represent shifty or aversive behaviour but it would be a significant leap to accuse that person of lying. Even lie detectors that measure the amount of sweat produced when you are asked questions while testing your blood pressure can be fooled by some accomplished liars. The message here, then, is to use your body language interpreting skills to decipher what you can, but also not to make huge assumptions. You could be terribly wrong and make the situation far worse than it already is.

Verbal 'tells'

Verbal communication is often referred to as a dance. It has a broad set of rules; I will speak for a minute or so while you listen, then I shall be quiet while you give your response for a minute or so, and so we go on taking it in turns, batting our comments back and forth like a polite tennis match. While the dance is adhered to, there is no problem, each of us knows our role and our place. However, if the dance is disrupted by either partner not dancing 'by the rules', perhaps by shouting, sulking, or not understanding the dance correctly (such as talking across each other or shouting to get attention rather than in anger), then confusion will break out.

Difficult verbal situations include those with people who shout and also those who are unnervingly quiet. Shouters tend to fall into two main types: those whose voices rise because they are excited or shout the odd command to make a point, and those who use continued shouting as an instrument of aggression. The former group use their voice for emphasis. They may shout at you but requesting that they moderate their tone will bring results because they are in control. The latter group are usually out of control, and are consequently not thinking straight. They have lost their tempers, are being aggressive and are caught up in a whirlwind of emotion. As mentioned previously, people who shout continually will eventually shout themselves out. They cannot sustain their anger at a high level and, as they now find themselves in a situation they cannot get out of easily, need to create a way of exiting the situation to save face. This is often done dramatically and with enormous flourish, such as a final fist shot on the table or slamming the door on their way out. Admittedly they may appear very scary at first, but it is often a very short interaction, and when you understand their tactics and the fact that it is actually they who are having trouble coping, you may feel secure in having the moral high ground.

Silent people are very different. It does not take much energy to be silent and so they can maintain their silence for a very long time. This, combined with the fact that they clearly have the most control over the situation, makes them much more difficult to deal with. Communication is essential to sort out life's problems and a refusal to speak shows obstinacy and a total lack of willingness to move towards a solution. Where you are faced with a wall of silence in a work situation, you will need to deal with it as a behavioural issue through your organisation's policies. Communication is essential in business and a refusal to communicate effectively may be a disciplinary issue.

Listening between the words

When we engage in any form of communication, we are listening to the words and taking in the body language, before computing the information through our own cultural filters in an attempt to make sense of the information. However, there is a third process that we also need to be aware of, one that is, perhaps, more instinctive. We rely so much on what people say and what we have observed that we forget to trust our own instincts and 'listen' between the words.

Listening to something that clearly is not there seems like a contradiction in terms, so let's examine the issues here. There are so many automatic utterances in our society. When asked, 'Hi, how are you?' most people will automatically reply 'Fine' in a fairly upbeat tone. There is nothing wrong with this; we all need short cuts to communicate in a fast way, and this is a very acceptable, and social, way of meeting and greeting. However, it does not really tell us anything of value about the other person.

Incongruence

Now, imagine the same response is given, but in monotone. There is automatically incongruence between the word 'Fine', which suggests that things are good, and the tone in which it is said. In this situation there is a danger that you hear the words, but do not take sufficient notice of the tone, thus losing the real meaning of the communication.

What is not being said?

Let's use a similar example. You ask, 'Does everyone agree that this is a good idea?' – two people say 'Yes' but the third does not respond. Their lack of response is lost as you concentrate on what you hoped to hear, and do not notice the silence from the third person. Their lack of affirmation needs to be checked out. Perhaps they did not hear you, or maybe they did not feel the need to respond, as the others replied sufficiently. But maybe, just maybe, they actually did not agree.

People do not respond for a number of reasons. It may be because they are shy or perhaps they do not feel able to openly disagree (they felt too pressured), or it could be because they need to think things through further. Whatever the reason, we cannot always assume that the less communicative people in the team are concurring with the other views being aired. They may have grave misgivings but choose to exhibit them later, when they might even cause more of a stir. If possible invite everyone individually to contribute to any decision by asking, 'Jim, we haven't heard from you yet. What do you think about the proposed change?'

Listening behind the message is vital if you want to truly connect with staff and be the most effective communicator you can ever be. Check out the words, the body language, and use your level of instinct to allow you to head off difficulties before they manifest into larger problems.

Look and learn

We have established that some people are more prone to visual and verbal 'tells' than others, and that these 'tells' may be exhibited in different ways. However, one thing we do know is that, unless people are made aware of these 'tells' or habits, they will continue to do them. They are amazingly consistent in the individual, with each individual displaying their own version of one or more anxiety tells. The lesson therefore is twofold. Firstly, pay close attention to the tells of others and make a mental note of them. You will then be in an excellent position to 'read' the emotions of your colleagues during a difficult interaction. Secondly, be very aware of your own signals. You may have others watching you and you may be giving too much away that is to their advantage.

Adjusting your own approach to build positive relationships

Right from the beginning I have stressed how important it is to recognise your own part in any dynamic. The other person may be exhibiting scary body language and may be coming right at you but how you present yourself and react will contribute towards a successful outcome.

Whatever the stance of the other person, make sure you present yourself using open body language. Meet the person square on and ensure you have good balance (this will give the impression of strength). Resist moving around too much or transferring weight from foot to foot through rocking movements (this can infer impatience with the other person). Imagine that you are a strong tree that is rooted into the ground. Perhaps you are an old Oak tree or a strong Yew. Not only do your roots give you strength but also they nourish and feed you. You feel powerful and grounded – ready to take on anything that the elements might throw at you.

Try to maintain a long posture with a straight back and an open chest. Restrict arm movements to those where impact is needed or when you need to drive messages home, but ensure that any contact arm movement, such as shaking hands or steering the other person by the elbow, is firm and decisive.

Maintain eye contact as much as possible and, if appropriate, display a slight smile. Listen, listen and listen again to what they are trying to tell you, and give nonverbal signals, such as the occasional nod, to show you are listening. Measure up other people's body language while not forgetting your own, and be prepared to shift and realign your body to ensure easier communication.

To learn more about this subject, read *Instant Manager: Body Language* by Geoff Ribbens and Greg Whitear and *Instant Manager: Neuro Linguistic Programming* by Mo Shapiro, available from Hodder Education.

Conclusion

We all move and interact with each other on a number of levels including subliminally. The main problem is that when we meet someone who is either being difficult or we know to be difficult, we forget to look for the signals that give us enhanced information regarding their temperament at that time. There are a number of very common 'tells' that reveal certain anxieties, and we can then change our approach in line with what is being exhibited. However, that anxiety may be there for a considerable number of different reasons, and we need good verbal communication if we want to reconcile any differences.

INSTANT TIP

Use all your senses, including intuition, to give yourself a head start in all your business relationships but cross reference as much as you can. Look for the subtle body language as well as the more obvious.

03

Difficult employees – how do I deal with them?

Sometimes when we become managers we are in the fortunate position of being able to select our team members, but more likely we may inherit a team. This could happen for a number of reasons: perhaps we are moving into a job where we are replacing the manager and the team is already in place, or it could be that we have been brought in as a new manager especially to take over a tricky team.

There is a third scenario, that the team is indeed new but the people in it are disaffected characters from other parts of the organisation. When forming a team all textbooks will tell you that it is essential to select the very best people, with the right skills. They are right, but unfortunately life is not always like a textbook and you may well find that the pool of people you have to choose from is very small, limited to those staff who are 'floating' in the organisation. Now, there may be a very good reason why they are not in permanent positions, and in no way should these people be rejected due to their circumstance, but you must consider that they may be disaffected. This either serves as a reason for their circumstance or they could be disaffected because of it. If this is the case, there could be hidden baggage of experience and emotion to contend with. This then means that you will have difficulties to deal with on top of the usual complexities experienced when taking over a team. However, as I mentioned earlier, you and your management style are heavily involved in the dynamic, and just because people have difficult employment history elsewhere does not mean that it will be repeated with you. The problem with bad reputations is that they follow people around for the rest of their lives, and may not be justified at all. Treat your new team or employees as a new blank canvas, and draw your own conclusions from their current behaviour, not the past.

Building the relationship right from the start

Not everyone comes to work to have a jolly time. Neither does everyone come to work brimming with enthusiasm every day. Although motivation to work is not entirely about money, there is no doubt that we need money in our lives to pay the bills. Money, then, plays a part, but so do other factors such as the human need to socialise and create bonds with others. There is also the need for people to work towards something – a goal – and feel that their work is noble in its move towards completing a project. We will look at motivation later but the money angle does not go away and it pays to be realistic about people if you are going to build a meaningful relationship with your employees.

At this point you may be thinking, 'What "relationship"? I am not planning on having a relationship with these people, I just work with them!' Well, like it or loathe it, you will be in a relationship with your staff, and from now on any interaction will be framed in the style of that relationship. So let's look at what we need in a relationship. We look for evidence of qualities such as:

- honesty
- reliability
- loyalty and
- camaraderie

to name just a few, and it is these qualities we will also be looking for in staff. Some of these will not be immediately evident in new employees therefore we need to invest in building that relationship to ensure that it is built on solid foundations.

Like all relationships, things can get off to a good or bad start, and this can set the tone for the rest of the relationship. This should not mean that you have to walk around as if on egg shells, but early actions leave lasting impressions that may be more difficult to erase later on. Far better to create a strong, positive force initially, than to have to try to salvage the situation later on.

Setting the 'personality' of your team

Leadership is essential and will help give your team or staff group a personality. What do I mean by personality? You must have noticed how some teams work better than others; how some staff members prefer to work for certain managers. Somehow working in one team can feel very different from working with another.

Figure 3.1: The team personality

There are three things you need to consider here:

- You – will have your own leadership style that you need to bring to the team (or your employees).
- The organisation – has its own personality (including its values) that you need to operate within.
- The team – when you introduce anyone new into an existing staff group, the dynamic will change.

Why is this important? Because all three factors combine to make up the team personally (see Figure 3.1) and the teams that have a feel good factor are the ones that never have a problem finding staff, in fact staff often clamber to join them. They run efficiently and effectively, and usually have low turnover of staff, thus saving your time later on recruitment. When staff start coming to you to ask when there might be vacancies in your team, you know you are working in the right direction.

Exercise

If you are unsure of the personality of your current staff mix, ask everyone. A team or group session is better than individual meetings for this topic, as it appears less subversive. Ask the staff to identify the team's strengths and areas for development. If you don't mind wacky, then ask the group, 'If we were an animal, what would our team be?' – or use a similar metaphor, and then extract the qualities. For example, it is of no benefit for anyone to say the team is like an elephant, without explaining how and why. From this data you can see whether this is the way you want to be represented. Ask everyone how they would like the team to be, and be open about everyone's role in making it happen.

This does not indicate soft leadership. In the same way that children like to know the boundaries, so do employees. Again, like children, they may push against them but clear working relations is very important in establishing the all important 'this is how we do things around here'. Either side of these boundaries, or organisational rules, there is considerable flex as to how the team is managed and its resulting personality.

Ensuring the right fit of role to success

As mentioned earlier, attracting the right staff to work with you is crucial, but not always possible. However, what you will find is that, as your ability to work well with people fuels your reputation, there will be people seeking you out and literally knocking on your door.

After a while, as your reputation grows, everyone will want to work for the manager who took on a difficult team and won them over.

Personalities aside you need to be sure that you have the right people in your team, and this is just as important for an established team as a new one. If you have a new team you can begin by sketching out exactly what role everyone is to have. These roles will become the basis for the future job descriptions (JD). Along with a JD you will also need a person specification (PS). The PS allows the manager to specify what kind of person they would like to undertake the role. The JD and the PS will form the basis of future recruitment, so it pays to ensure they are right and that you have designed a mix of people for your team. Don't be tempted to take a blanket approach and think that you want everyone to be 'enthusiastic, lively and outgoing' when in fact having some people who are 'conscientious, thoughtful and detail conscious' would also be welcome to provide balance. You could easily end up with a team of people who are all the same and, far from being harmonious, that could be the cause of difficulty!

If you are inheriting a team or group of employees you may think that you can do little except carry on where the previous manager left off. Absolutely not – if you always do what you always did, you will always get what you always got. Time for a total rethink and it is back to roles once again. How would you like your team or staff to be organised? What would work best for the business? Do certain roles need more interaction than others?

Now let's look at who you have, their experience, qualifications and their personalities and preferences – and this means talking to everyone both individually and as a team. Keep the dialogue open and fluid. You know that people work best when they:

- use their skills and knowledge
- work in teams where they are respected
- feel they can achieve
- get regular feedback on their performance

... so, as far as possible you want to match them to a role that provides this.

What about when you want to change the roles of staff, but can't? Firstly, speak with your own manager about this. Essentially you are being asked to manage with one arm tied behind your back, and your lack of influence on the roles will mean that you cannot be held totally responsible for the outcome. This can be very frustrating for you as well as your staff. However, if this is the case you also need to be totally clear with your employees, and ask for their support. Being clear and honest gives them choices – the choice to stick in there or walk away. Losing staff is never helpful but the worst scenario is not that someone leaves, it is that employees stay, but become disillusioned. If this happens, maintain all levels of honesty and openness. This is the situation and you need to remember that you are not responsible for how others feel about it. If their behaviour becomes problematic you will need to deal with this in the same way as you would deal with any other displays of difficult behaviour. When it comes to behaviour, we all have choices and all choices come with consequences. We all need to be responsible for the consequences that result from our choice of behaviour.

Matching motivation

The right cognitive approach is also essential. We all come to work for different reasons and others may not be as motivated as ourselves, or at least motivated by the same things. You may be excited by being a new manager and keen to try out some of your theories, but your employees may be feeling apprehensive. After all, you are an unknown quantity for them, and there is a common perception that all change is negative. You will be seen as the change maker, and this could cause a temporary barrier between you and your staff.

You need to find out more about your employees. Why do they come to work? Apart from the obvious financial benefit, what do they personally gain from being there? Who do they interact with/lunch with? What aspects of the job do they like/dislike? Where do they hope to go in their career? How do they think you can help them get there?

This 'getting to know you' approach will not just help to give you broad information about your employees but will specifically target their motivation drivers. When you know what brings people into work, you can build some of that into their day-to-day working environment. Don't be fooled by the answer 'Money', as that is only ever half of the story. People are essentially social animals, yes, even introverts. Being around people is a very basic human need, and as many people come to work to join an interactive social entity as come to avoid a lonely or emotionally dull home life. It has been identified that home workers can easily become isolated so it is important that they are connected with others, even if it is through a buddying system, periodic team meetings, visits or Internet contact.

Whether we like it or not our work defines us. What is one of the first things that people ask each other when they first meet? Where do you work? Or, what do you do? It says a lot about who we are and how we operate, and therefore it is important to get it right. If the motivation is absent from work, employees will not only enter work in the most unproductive manner, but will also be telling their friends that they don't enjoy working there. When you think of how much your company spends on advertising, telling the world that it is a great company to work for, that could be very damaging. If employees really don't like where they work or the work they do, although a hard message, it is far better that they go and work somewhere else.

The motivation and behaviour discussed here has mostly been about your employees, and the temptation is to think that, once again, this is about other people. However, real behavioural change starts with ourselves. How can we expect good behaviour in others when not displaying it ourselves? Modelling motivational behaviour is important in showing others what is expected. Pick up almost any book concerned with self improvement at work and you will see that it advises the reader to copy the styles of managers they admire. The message is to dress and act yourself into a senior role, therefore making it very easy for any future employer to see you in that new light, and smooth the transition. Now think about your current employees. Are you modelling winning behaviour and language? Managers can so easily be found modelling the behaviour that they then moan about in staff. Hold the mirror up to yourself and see how your motivation displays itself, before blaming others. This concept is covered in greater detail in Chapter 9.

Personality profiling

The idea that people can operate in a set number of ways that enable others to predict their behaviour is not new. Thousands of years ago the Greeks used a system of four humours to describe personality types:

- Sanguine – the Artisan, courageous, hopeful and amorous
- Melancholic – the Rationalist, despondent, sleepless and irritable
- Phlegmatic – the Idealist, calm and unemotional
- Choleric – the Guardian, easily angered and bad tempered.

Do you recognise yourself or any of your employees in that list? It is probably a bit basic for our current level of understanding about people, but it does give an indication that, even at that time, it had been noticed that human behaviour tended to fall into discrete categories.

More recently modern psychologists have devised further categorisation. In the early 1940s Raymond Cattell began by taking no fewer than 17,953 trait labels, then grouping them into clusters that shared their meaning. This produced 171 clusters. He reduced these to twenty and then, finally, to sixteen, which he incorporated into the first edition of his famous personality questionnaire. Much work was undertaken by his contemporaries, and also later psychologists, and the result is five scales that nearly all personality questionnaires now include as the basis of their interpretation. These five scales are known as the Big Five, and measure:

- Extroversion
- Neuroticism/Anxiety
- Openness to experience/Conformity
- Agreeableness/Tender vs Tough-mindedness
- Conscientiousness.

Whereas we do not want to 'box' people, some information concerning your employee's personality type could be very useful for helping you to know the best way to manage them. For example, knowing that you have a number of introverted staff, you might consider putting suggestion boxes in prominent places for ideas, rather than simply relying on ideas emerging in meetings or open forums, where introverts may feel ill at ease.

So is it a good idea to put everyone through a personality questionnaire? They have a dual purpose: you learn more about your staff but, perhaps even more importantly, they learn more about themselves. Self-knowledge leaves an open door for dealing with difficult behaviour. When anyone is curious to discover more about themselves, it is a good time to discuss how their behaviour also affects the people around them. Sometimes a conversation opener is what we need to approach an uncomfortable issue.

If personality profiles could help you and your employees, then better be safe than sorry, and being safe means using:

- a well-documented testing procedure – never buy a product off the shelf. It will not have been subjected to the rigorous testing of the major tests
- a practitioner who can advise and run the tests for you – all tests do not measure the same aspects of personality and therefore you need to know that you are measuring the traits that you have identified as being useful in the job role. A practitioner needs to hold a Level B certificate in psychometrics to ensure they are aware not only of how the test operates but also are able to give high quality interpretation of the results and provide feedback. A list of registered practitioners can be obtained from the British Psychological Society (BPS).

Never try to cut corners by using tests without expert help. Should you subsequently find yourself accused of constructive dismissal, or in an Employment Tribunal, the fact that you were dabbling in areas you are not qualified in will stand against you.

When used correctly and with sufficient support, psychometric tests can open up a whole new dialogue around how we are the way we are and why we do things in the way that we do. They can help us understand ourselves and others, and also help to look at groups of people, such as team mix. When they are used in a positive way they enable everyone to look at their strong areas, while also identifying areas of our personality that need some development.

Your organisation has a personality too. Inherently it will favour certain characteristics and reward them accordingly. Think for a moment – does your organisation favour those who are more extrovert or those more introvert? Does it value sparky, lively people or thinkers? Does it like risk takers, or risk averse characters? It is good to consider, for your future progression, how you fit into the personality of your organisation. A good match and your long-term future is assured, but less of a match may require future development.

Identifying personal influencers

In every group there are influencers and disrupters, and in some sense the qualities they bring to each of these roles are similar. In essence these people have some form of people power in that they are able to influence others, sometimes positively and sometimes negatively. After all, if they had no influence and were ignored, they would not be able to stir things up for either good or bad.

French and Ravens (1960) identified the following power bases:

- Reward power: the ability to give or take away praise, resources, funding, promotion.
- Coercive power: the ability to punish and reprimand.
- Legitimate power: from one's position or office.
- Expert power: the use of superior knowledge and skills.
- Referent power: where others seek the leader's approval.
- Information power: to give, withhold or filter information.
- Connection power: perceived to be in close contact with influential people.
- Ascribed power: accurate or distorted attributions of power ascribed to another person.

Exercise

See whether you are able to identify staff who are highly influential or disruptive in your team. How does their behaviour manifest itself? What do you think you can do about this behaviour?

The reason for identifying the power play in employee groups is to tap into their skills and work with them rather than against them. Let's think firstly of our influencer. Let's call her Sasha. Sasha works hard and is very popular with the other staff. She always seems to know what is happening and what she is doing. In the past she has trained other employees and run induction programmes for new employees. In the model above, Sasha has ascribed power, given to her by others – but she also now has information power. She therefore has a high level of influence that we can use as a communication pathway. In this instance you could ask Sasha to help you with a new change project that has recently been announced. Brief her fully so that she has all the facts and mention that you will be consulting on it at the next team meeting, when you hope everyone will be present to hear the outcome. Sasha will sell the idea for you and, because of her position of power, will be more convincing and influential than you would be. You will be sure of a full house at the team meeting!

When you allow influencers to do their work, it is crucial that you do not intervene or make your own announcement. You need to back off and allow them time and space to weave their magic web. For the manager, this letting go might not seem natural. You may feel that you would rather wade in and exert your own personality as manager. After all, you have the most current appreciation of the situation. But resist. Allow your influencer to do the hard work for you and you may find that when it comes to the meeting, the people in front of you are already half way to being persuaded of the idea, and just need your final comments to add authority.

Now let's think about Petra. She's a passive-aggressive so spreads her disruption through snide comments, sarcasm and put downs. Whether she wants these new changes or not, if she finds out about them first, she will lay down her poison – remember that she is still influential but in a negative way. Other employees still listen to her, possibly for entertainment (because it can be funny sometimes to see her launch off), but also to hear her 'version' of events. If the other staff buy into her behaviour, she will also have ascribed power, and so we don't want to add information power to her portfolio.

To start with we will handle this behaviour in the here and now, and look at the longer term issues of Petra's behaviour in a moment. In the first instance, you need to make sure that the message is pure. This means that everyone will hear or read (preferably both) the same message, and they will not get Petra's spin on things prior to the event. Decide how you will communicate the message, and when it is to be released (timing). This puts you totally in control.

When you give the message about the changes, ask for everyone's attention and remind them that you will answer questions only at the end. It you see Petra either whispering or gesturing, put her on the spot: 'Petra, you seem anxious to tell us something, would you like to tell everyone what it is?' If Petra truly is a passive-aggressive she will not want to be exposed in this way, and will be quiet. If so, ask her to come and see you privately later. If she blurts out something aggressive, such as, 'Well, we all know this is about cut backs, no matter how management dress it up', thank her for her comment and point out that this is only one person's view of the situation, and that yours is totally different (you may want to add here that you are more likely to have the most up-to-date information, so it may be worth everyone concentrating on that), continue the meeting and then ask to meet with Petra later.

Let us return to unpicking the above situation. It is made up of two sections: Petra's views regarding the change, and her behaviour. Figure 3.2 demonstrates where there should be management action or intervention.

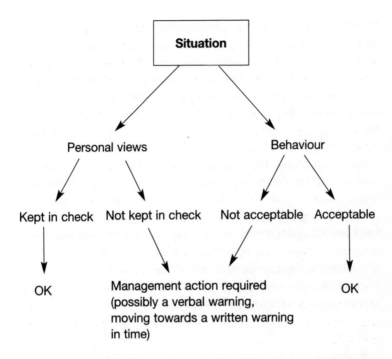

Figure 3.2: Activity on Node example

Everyone is entitled to their views regarding any work decision, but they are not entitled to disrupt the entire team because of those views. Although there are many unwritten rules governing our behaviour, a level of social behaviour is expected in the workplace. You may even have a charter naming some such behaviours, represented as 'respect for others' or similar codes of conduct. In many organisations, acting in an antisocial manner or displaying poor or disruptive behaviour is considered misconduct.

Petra's behaviour should be taken very seriously. Bad behaviour that is allowed to continue, rather than be addressed, sets a precedence for any future behaviour in the workforce. Some people actually need to be told directly that their behaviour is not acceptable because they just don't realise. For example, if you came from a family who habitually swear, then you would consider that to be a normal way of communicating. As a manager, turning a blind eye is simply not an option otherwise the situation will be ten times more difficult to address in the future. If performance management is being exercised through regular one-to-ones and an appraisal system, target setting should be part of the culture. Targets can be set for behaviour as well as work output, and a written record of the meeting should always be kept. In the example above, I would set Petra some very tight targets around her behaviour and monitor her against them fairly regularly. By doing this I am outwardly demonstrating that I am on her case and if she slips into this behaviour again I should feel more able to remind her of her targets, thereby taking control of the situation. In empowering yourself to deal with this type of situation effectively, Petra will be disempowered in her poor behaviour.

Exercise

Find out NOW your organisation's policy on performance management, and get advice regarding what is and is not considered acceptable conduct.

Conclusion

You may have a team of diverse employees but you need to use your skill to identify difficult behaviour and deal with it. Really get to know your employees as individuals, find out their career histories, their motivations, and their personalities. Always look for a reason behind poor behaviour and consider whether it is justified or not. If it is not and it is the first occasion, have a quiet word. If it has happened a couple of times, set targets, but if it is an ongoing problem it must be picked up through the correct organisational procedure. If you have to go down this route, make sure you keep a written record of all the incident times, and the measures you took at each point on the way. This would be your evidence if necessary.

INSTANT TIP

Really get to know your employees. There may be reasons behind their behaviour that you, as a manager, are in a position to change. Feel in control of the situation and use organisational policies to help support your actions.

04

Difficult managers – how do I deal with them?

Some of the biggest problems may not lie with the people you are managing but in your managers and senior managers. It may be that they:

- feel in a position of superiority and choose to exert their influence inappropriately
- communicate very poorly
- are complete workaholics
- are 'old school' and have decided that they have no need to know about being a manager in the twenty-first century
- feel unable to let go or delegate work to others who may help them to achieve – but they perceive as a threat.

There is no doubt that managers are in a superior position, and therefore in a position of power – with the power to ultimately hire and fire employees. It may also be that they own the organisation or have been senior there for a very long time. If your manager owns the organisation or company, and is behaving very badly to you, you need to think very clearly whether you really want to work for someone like that. Not only will they continue to treat you poorly but there is also the danger that you may slip into the practice of thinking this is natural, and therefore develop a similar style, to fit the culture. This would be such a shame as it would render you a less attractive proposition to any other, more enlightened organisations, and therefore limit your career possibilities in the future. An organisation's culture is linked to its reputation and is often known far and wide. Your decision to work within that culture says a lot about you and your values. If the fit is wrong, you may find that it is not only the manager you are trying to distance yourself from, but also your association with that company.

The manager/worker relationship

Essentially the employer/employee relationship is one of a work-for-wage bargain. You will provide the work and for that you will receive a wage – all other facets of the job are open for negotiation. Employment law is also clear that you are entitled to guidance and training in aspects of your job and you, as a manager, have a duty of care for the staff who report to you. Your manager, however senior, also has this responsibility. Although it is not wise to remind your manager of this point, it is worth bearing in mind should any problems arise later in your relationship.

Everyone has within them a source of personal power, but only some of us choose to use that power effectively or even appropriately. Within the context of difficult managers, identifying and strengthening our own personal power can help us gain the strength to deal with difficult situations. You will remember that we discussed different types of power in the previous chapter. Your manager may have legitimate power due to their position in the hierarchy but it is an external value, and one that you ascribe them. Legitimate power can be gained and lost in an instant, leaving the person with nothing. Personal power comes from within, can be made stronger and developed. Yes it can be dented, but it does not disappear and every knock back can result in it being stronger than before. Every difficult situation you encounter with a manager is a learning opportunity, a chance to be better next time. At the end of each day, however difficult the day has been, the most important thing is that you can reflect on each situation and know that you took the very best possible decisions and actions.

To strengthen your personal power core:

- Let go of blame and guilt both for yourself and towards others. When in a crisis it is better to deal with the situation at hand, rather than looking for a handle to hang blame on to.
- Be forgiving. Everyone has the means to be passive, manipulative and aggressive, and your manager may be pushed to their absolute limit at that particular time. Often this comes from feeling cornered or being resentful. Allow them to be human and demonstrate their weaknesses, then move them forward into joint problem solving. It may be that you can work on a problem together.
- Learn how to back off from a disagreement without becoming aggressive, even if the other person is. Leaving a confrontation with, 'I need to go now so I'm afraid we must agree to differ on that point,'

is far more empowering than fighting to the end. It also enables the other person, possibly someone more senior than yourself, room to withdraw with good grace.

- Don't apologise for anything that is not your fault. It can be very tempting to become the professional scapegoat, but it will demonstrate to others that you are very weak. The more that you are willing to shoulder the blame for someone else, the more others will take advantage of this. There is one exception here: if a member of your team has made a mistake then it is accepted that, as team manager, you share some, or all, of that outcome.

- Shake off any feelings you have about winning or losing with your manager. You should be working together effectively, not in a combative relationship. Playing at 'who wins or loses' can become petty and distract you both from the real business you should be concentrating on.

- Be firm in your values, beliefs and feelings. Each of us has a personal code that we live by and we should feel proud of that. If we see someone being bullied, we should speak up, or risk being complicit in that situation. People who can stand up for others and their own views, however unpopular, will find that they gain an inner boost to their personal power in knowing that what they did was right.

- Learn and move on. There is nothing worse than making mistakes only to repeat the errors twelve months down the line. People forgive others who learn from their mistakes, but have little time for those who keep repeating the same patterns of bad behaviour.

Consider the relationship between yourself and other managers (not just your own) very carefully.

- How do you interact with each other?
- What happens when you meet? (Not just at a superficial level – what body language is displayed?)
- When you speak do you look each other in the eye?
- How are requests/orders given? In what manner?
- What happens when things go wrong?
- How are problems reported to you and what are the likely penalties?

The answer to these questions will tell you about your relationship with senior staff and how they relate to you and your position. Be clear to separate the two. Senior staff may have negative (or positive) feelings about you, or about all managers at your grade – it is helpful to know whether these feelings are personal or not, as they may affect your actions.

What can you do to help build bridges in the relationship? Here are some first steps:

- Act quietly confident. If you really don't know something then, of course, ask. However, do not ask questions about areas of business in the assumption that you will automatically flatter senior staff by their ability to answer them. There is always the possibility that senior managers will assume that you should already know a certain amount of information and, if you do not, then you may have been a poor choice for the job.
- However, when you want to ask, then ask with confidence. Like a salesperson, you need your

manager to feel good about saying yes. People like to be challenged with dynamic questions that demonstrate that the querent knows a good deal about the underlying issues of the business. For example, instead of asking, 'How will the current market affect our sales over the next five years?' a better phrasing of the question might be, 'Given the increase in the price of oil and the strength of the Euro against the pound, are there any specific strategies for sales being put in action to see the company through the next five years?' Although more wordy, the second example demonstrates that you know a good deal more about the situation than the first. Never be afraid to ask for favours either. People are happy to help out those they like, if they think the result will be worth the time investment.

● Try to be personable. Reflect on any feedback you may have had in the past – whether you agreed with the giver or not, they may have had a point. While it is not always necessary to like others, people are more likely to be open in their communication with you if they like you. Don't forget rapport building techniques such as asking someone how they are when you meet, or how their day is going – it helps to build an instant connection.

● Phrase your question as a request for shared activity. Asking someone to problem solve alongside you is very flattering at any level as it shows acknowledgement of their skills and experience. Instead of asking your own manager, 'How can I motivate my staff?' try suggesting, 'I would like to discuss with you some more ideas for motivating staff. I have my own ideas, but together I thought we may come up with some additional methods I could introduce.' Again, the second sentence makes you appear less needy and more in control of the situation, while simultaneously suggesting that the other person may have a great deal to offer to the conversation.

The view from the top

Every level of management has a different view. Imagine you are climbing a high tower. The view at the bottom would be seeing people and buildings life-sized, as people go about their daily work. If you moved half way up that tower, the people would be smaller and you would see less detail but you would be able to get an aerial view – and you just might be able to see where those people were scurrying off to. Higher up the tower and again the view becomes different. There is even less detail and you might not be able to identify particular people; they might all look like ants! From this view you can also see farther and wider into the distance; you may be able to see the end of land and where it becomes sea, or where the city peters out to become countryside. At the top of the tower you will just have a large overview of everything and everyone. The people are not necessarily now seen as individuals, and rather than being concerned by where each person goes, you would be able to see patterns of mass migration.

This analogy is the same in business. As managers move up in the organisation their 'view' becomes different. They may lose some of the individualism and concentrate more on the larger picture, for example, how the organisation is placed in the open market. It is important to be aware of this change of view because it affects not only you for the future, but also your dealings with senior managers, and it may explain why some of your communications have not been successful. Perhaps you are just not appreciating each other's 'view' and something that seems important to you may not even appear on a more senior manager's radar.

Remember: If you want to appeal to your manager for something, it is far better to couch the request in terms of their view of the world. For example, asking for new chairs for my team may not interest my manager and I may be brushed off, but couch it in terms of supporting the health and safety check that is happening next month, and my manager will be far more willing to listen because that falls more into their strategic role.

The other point here is that as soon as you become a manager or supervisor you become the filling in a sandwich. In other words, until that moment you only had to concern yourself with what your manager said and how your manager or supervisor felt about you and your work. As soon as you move up one rung and become that manager or supervisor, that is when you become the filling. By this I mean that suddenly you need to be aware of not only the manager above you but also the workforce or team below you in the hierarchy. You are suddenly managing both up and down. This is particularly evident when it comes to information. You have to become a filter. Your manager above you does not want or need to know every nuance about the staff in your care, and likewise you will not be passing on every word your manager says, down to the team. (You will not want to clog the team with information that they either do not want, or need, to know.) You may indeed become your manager's confidante, but part of working together, and building trust includes not passing that information on. There are no hard and fast rules about what information you should and should not share, and most managers are expected to learn this trick as they go along. Unfortunately, on occasions, this can also be the cause of difficult situations, for example if the wrong information is communicated either up or down the organisation. If in doubt, never share information, especially personal or sensitive information, unless cleared with everyone concerned.

Remember: Be guarded in the information you pass on and be aware that the view, and therefore business focus, is very different from different levels in the organisation. When your manager looks at you blankly it could be because they do not understand why you have come to them with this information. It just might not be relevant to them.

At different levels, in addition to the differing priorities mentioned above, there are also differing pressure points and deadlines. You may be working to a weekly output plan but your direct manager may be working on an annual rolling programme, which requires different measuring and forecasting procedures. You may be happy if you go home at the end of the week with your team having met their targets for that period; your manager may be living under continual stress to deliver and perform on a schedule that appears to have no end. Again, this could have you discussing seemingly common issues while having different levels of understanding and anxiety. It is often here that difficultly once more creeps into the equation, where you see a senior manager as doing less tactical work than yourself, and delegating many tasks to more junior staff or managers such as yourself. On the other hand your manager feels that you have the easier job: dealing with short-term, easily measurable goals and not having responsibility for ultimate success or failure of the project, large budgets and securing the jobs of everyone in the division.

Exercise: Part A

Divide a piece of paper in half lengthways. On one side list your main duties, targets and outcomes. Now on the other, take a guess at those of your immediate manager. Now look at the two lists and see where the pressure points are and where you could be communicating at odds. How can you communicate in a way that will bring empathy and understanding from your manager to your own work? Perhaps you can appeal to their prior experience (if they have been promoted), and ask them how they used to handle situations, when they did your job.

Exercise: Part B

Go back to your original lists and now look for commonalities. Where are the areas where either you and your manager both have joint concerns/responsibilities, or there may be a link? It might be that you both share the same outcomes of a project or that a piece of work you are doing fulfils his or her overarching work schedule. When you start to see how your work links directly with your manager's you will be able to communicate better, giving them the level of detailed information they require.

To improve communication further you need to learn to speak in their own language as much as possible. If you need to raise a tactical issue, tie it in to one of your manager's outcomes. For example, if you wanted to speak to your manager about two workers constantly disagreeing, your manager may immediately think that you really should not be bothering them with such inconsequential piffle and should sort it out yourself. However, when you raise it as a concern that the end of quarter targets may not be met, then you will definitely have them listening! If you need your manager to listen to you, think through how you will phrase the message so that you capture their attention in the most effective method possible.

The other point here is to consider in detail how you present your information, such as phrasing information in as positive manner as possible. Your boss will have so many problems that another one will simply get them down and you may be on the receiving end of that emotion. Therefore, without being glib or inappropriate, try to demonstrate the positive side of any situation. For example, rather than saying, 'It looks like Jim might be late with the report figures for tomorrow because they are so much more difficult than usual' and getting both you and Jim bawled out you could try, 'The new frameworks for the figures will lead us to a much more accurate assessment of where we are making positive changes, however, they seem to be taking a little longer than before and therefore, there may be a slight delay in getting them to you this week. If this continues to be a problem, can I suggest that we design a longer lead-in time to enable Jim to do a good job? I'm sure you will think the result is worth the extra time.' You may still get bawled out but it is unlikely Jim will be, and he will be forever grateful to you. The second approach also provides your manager with a softer approach that they can then repeat to their manager. Remember to sell the message upwards and protect your staff in the process. There is always the possibility that you can 'sell' a mistake as an opportunity, and your staff will respect you for protecting them.

Internal politics

Internal politics are a fact of life. In many large companies managers need to position and reposition themselves constantly, and work can be an ever-changing landscape. It does not help that decisions do not always appear to be rational. You may feel that you are doing a good job and communicating well, only to be replaced by someone else. It therefore always pays to keep one eye on the horizon and build in some of your own support mechanisms. Three ideas to help are:

- Build a support group – this could be a networking group at a professional or personal level. Everyone needs to let off steam from time to time and it is better you do this with someone other than your manager.
- Find a mentor – a mentor will help you not only by supporting you but also offering advice, help and information. They are experienced people who have

probably been in the same situation that you are in now,
and they want to help you.
- Work to improve your skills level – this will give you
  knowledge and instant confidence. One additional bonus
  is that any extra skills can be taken with you should it be
  necessary to leave the organisation.

When vast changes take place in organisations, most of the staff
will start aligning themselves with whoever is the new power base.
You need to think very carefully before you fully align your
allegiance in any one direction (some organisations are more
political than a Tudor court). Complicating the matter is that you
may have very strong views that lead you in one direction and these
may be unpopular. People can be much admired for their strength
of view or vision but you need to be aware that you will be judged
by that. If your view conflicts very strongly with your manager's,
it can be a long and lonely fight. If that happens, you might be better
to take your ideas somewhere else – only you will know.

Conflict with your boss is not very comfortable and you may
need to ask yourself whether you need this level of hassle. Some of
this will depend on how important the job is to you.

The model in Figure 4.1 shows four segments. Firstly, you need
to decide whether the job you have is of high or low importance to
you. There are times when we are stuck in our job for reasons that
are meaningful only to ourselves. Perhaps we have to be in that job
because of the kudos that goes with it, or even the money. Our job
role links directly to our status and therefore it may be that we
cannot move out without losing face – after all once you have made
it to senior management, no one wants to hear you bleating about
how stressful it is.

The second stage is to decide whether you are experiencing
high or low levels of managerial conflict. If managerial conflict is too
high it can cause stress and all manner of associated disorders
such as high blood pressure, digestive and muscular problems.

	High importance	Low importance
High levels of managerial conflict	You could feel like you are on an emotional rollercoaster. You may have to hang in there for your job and find coping mechanisms.	Look around for another job. You are being subjected to large amounts of negative conflict for no apparent gain.
Low levels of managerial conflict	You may be able to work in harmony here but make sure you instigate some creative thinking to introduce some spark.	You may want to stay if you value harmony but this role will not take your career further.

Figure 4.1: Level of importance

However, if there are very low levels of managerial conflict you may need to ask yourself whether there is enough 'spark' at that level and whether anyone is prepared to challenge each other.

Some people thrive on a challenging atmosphere and others do not. For this reason you also need to consider your own personality and preference. We are all different in the amount of pressure we can work with, and also what we deem to be pressure-causing situations. One person's crushing pressure is another person's stimulating workplace.

The key here is to work with your own levels. There are many different organisations and styles of working, and therefore if one organisation is not right for you, there are others that might be a better fit.

Coping or escaping – what's it to be?

There are going to be times when you feel that the relationship you have with your own manager is not going to be workable due to their behaviour. Whatever type of difficult behaviour is being displayed, as long as it is not violent, you need to decide how to deal with it (see Figure 4.2).

In Figure 4.2, the first question deals with whether or not you can have an open and honest conversation with your manager. If they are continually difficult, this may not be possible, and will render any kind of logical, structured, conversation very difficult. The second consideration, then is whether the situation is likely to change. If your manager is going through a hard time, perhaps a personal situation such as divorce or family problems, there is a chance that these may sort themselves out in time. Even difficult work situations do eventually level out, and if this is the case, it might be worth seeing the situation for what it is – a temporary problem that will eventually fizzle out – and your manager may even feel grateful to you for hanging in there. The alternative is to leave, and it may be that this is the best course of action. However, this may not be so simple if you are 'trapped' in your job due to it being:

- a family run business
- an organisation with a brilliant reputation for your career (but a lousy culture)
- the only company in your area that specialises in this business area.

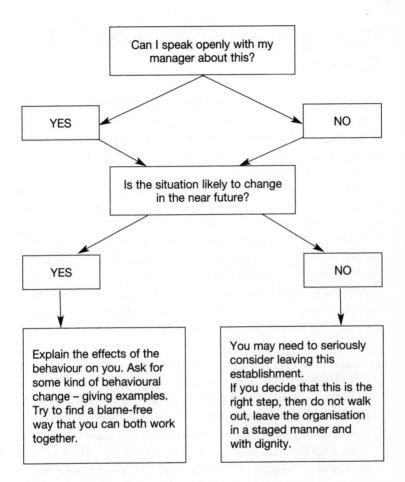

Figure 4.2: Coping or escaping – what is it to be?

Note: If the behaviour is violent in any way, please make sure that you take expert advice or report any incidents.

If any of these are the case then you cannot just leave and in reality we are looking at coping mechanisms until something change or your manager leaves. Earlier in this chapter I mentioned using a mentor, and in Chapter 5 I detail the merits of a mentor, and how mentoring operates. Mentors can be great at enabling you to cope with a difficult manager, and hang in there while others flee. However, the mentors mentioned were internal to the organisation. Sometimes this is less helpful than a totally independent view, which is what you will get from an external mentor.

To locate an external mentor, in the first instance try contacting any professional body you may belong to. If that draws a blank, try your local Business Link or Chamber of Commerce, and see whether they have a mentoring scheme you could join. If these are all unsuccessful, you could try approaching another manager from another company – just make sure it is not one of your competitors!!

Throughout this book we will look at some case studies to give you practice of dealing with difficult people. Suggested solutions are to be found at the end of the book, pages 175–184.

Case study 1

Bob Lucas works at National Fuel and has always worked under Phil Williams who is a very supportive manager. He has just moved department to work under Pete Jones because Pete is heading up a new project, and Bob thinks that working on it would look good on his CV. From the moment he starts, he realises that Pete's style is very different to Phil's, and Bob is finding working with him very difficult. Pete does not tell Bob about the outcome of meetings, he is disorganised and shouts at the team. Bob does not want to change jobs again so he needs to think of ways of coping. What would you do if you were Bob?

Case study 2

Poona Sinclair has just started at Precision Computers. It is her first job and her boss, Linda Grace, was very nice at the interview but is turning out to be not at all what Poona expected. Linda is bossy and rude, and she makes racist comments to Poona (who is from Asia). Poona very quickly realises that she does not want to stay there any longer but feels weak for running away, and it will look odd on her CV. Perhaps all bosses are like this. As a friend, what would you advise her to do?

Conclusion

Having a difficult manager or boss puts you in a very tricky situation. You may not have known their true personality or management style when you joined the company. You have only three main options: coping, leaving, or changing your style to suit the company. What you decide will depend very much on a number of factors and will be a very personal decision. Although in your heart you may want to move on life is not always so clear cut and there may be limited options. For this reason, and because you may move somewhere else with a boss equally as difficult (but perhaps in a different way), it pays to consider trying out some coping skills. They will stand you in good stead for dealing with so many different situations in your future career.

INSTANT TIP

Read business plans and forecasts to find out the pressure points for your boss or any of the senior managers. Link your work to these as much as possible and try to work with their frustrations rather than dismiss them.

05

Difficult colleagues – how do I deal with them?

The colleague relationship can be fraught with difficulty in itself. For a start your work colleagues, unlike friends in real life, are not necessarily people you choose to be with. You have to be productive together to get the work done, even if, on occasions, you feel that your skills and knowledge are superior to theirs. If that isn't enough you also have to keep one eye out for 'game play' where they may be after your job or, what you had considered to be, your natural progression. Yes, when it comes to work colleagues you can be working alongside them one week and for them the following week. There is an old saying, 'Be nice to the people on the way up because you might meet them again on the way down!'

The colleagues we are discussing here could be anyone from the people you meet at work to those you bring into the organisation to work alongside you. Perhaps you share an office or work near each other, or maybe you could have been put together to work on a project. Whatever the situation, or however you met, you all have a vested interest in the relationship. Work colleagues can be a great source of support and help but equally they can also cause a lot of anxiety.

Creating the right atmosphere at work

One of the biggest mistakes that people make with colleagues is to underestimate how their relationship affects the atmosphere at work. Although we don't go to work expecting to be happy all the time, working in an atmosphere of mistrust and suspicion can grind anyone down. It is not just you who is affected either. Staff working for you will sense the atmosphere and this may have an impact on their motivation. Similarly your manager may also sense something is wrong and may just side with the other person, leaving you feeling let down, unsupported and isolated.

It might be worth spending just a few moments thinking about what constitutes a bad atmosphere for you. Is it about people not speaking or speaking too much? Is it about having the wrong people around you every day? Or perhaps it is about a lack of respect or suspicion? Bad atmospheres are like poison and can make your day not only unproductive but unendurable. Whatever the right atmosphere is for you, you need to be able to identify it in some way if you are going to do anything about it.

Ask yourself another set of questions, such as how would you like your working environment to be? Some people like air conditioning, others don't. For some people music in the background is soothing, for others it is an irritant. Some like to work in incredibly beautiful surroundings or buildings with character, while for others it is the type of people one surrounds one's self with that is important. It all adds to the atmosphere at work.

If you like great ideas and a 'buzzing' feel to your day you need to surround yourself (or at least be able to get your 'fix' at some point during the day) with creative and 'happening' people. Negative colleagues will drain you, over-excitable colleagues will tire you in the long term, and overly playful colleagues may be better restricted to small doses. Think about your colleagues not only in the sense of 'do I like them?' but also in the sense of 'do they provide the atmosphere, ambiance and stimulation I need to excel in my job?'. Atmosphere is as much about the people you work with, as the décor.

Exploring your relationship

Now let's consider the curse of the 'Return of the Colleague'. Okay, so you joined at the same time on the graduate scheme, or perhaps you worked together on that tricky project a couple of years ago. Now you are going to be working together again and it will be just the same, won't it? Or perhaps it will be even better.

People change. Time, life and experience change us all and most people will have had different experiences even in just one year that may radically impact on the way in which they work. Coupled with the fact that there may now be even more competition between you, or a power imbalance in some way, and we are set for fireworks.

You may find you previously worked well together on separate projects with different managers but now you are flung together and you start to suspect that you never really knew the other person at all. Don't expect relationships to stay the same. The likelihood is that you will have moved on and so will they: you are back to the beginning, starting over and need to forge a new relationship. The good thing is that, if you are both able to be honest, knowing each other from the past can make a good base for the future. You can openly acknowledge where you have come from in life's journey, but you may want to be more guarded as to your future – just in case.

It is always difficult when friends become competitors and it is a mistake to believe that it will not change your relationship, no matter what they may say. However, use your prior history to talk things through. They are probably just as nervous as you about the situation.

Identifying what's in it for them

Behaviour is governed by our wants and needs. Freud postulated the concept of the 'pleasure principle', and our base need to satisfy this need. Freud would say that this need is a driver that governs all our decisions. What gives us pleasure is what we do. Even altruism, the act of selflessly putting others first, Freud would argue is governed by the pleasure principle. He would say that by putting others first, you were gaining satisfaction, the satisfaction of knowing that you have helped. So it is difficult to get away from this concept.

Later behavioural psychologists have worked on this principle and used it to train animals, calling it 'reward' strategy. In essence animals can be trained to do certain movements due to the fact that they are given a reward. It is no surprise that the reward has to be something of value to them, or something they covet, to make them do as you wish. It is from this that we have evolved reward strategies at work – sell so many widgets, meet your target, and you will get your reward. This idea has permeated society as a whole, and we happily collect vouchers, coupons, or continue to shop in the same store to collect a reward of some kind. Reward buys repeat behaviour, as long as the purchaser values the reward.

Now let's link this reward to emotions by trying a little exercise. Close your eyes and imagine feeling really good. It does not matter where or when, just the intensity of the feelings. Try to feel that intensity of pleasure throughout your entire body, from the top of your head to the tips of your toes. Now try to imagine that feeling ten times more intense, ten times more colourful, and ten times more pleasurable. Finally, link that feeling to a situation you don't much like, perhaps eating a certain vegetable or your rush hour trip in to work. See yourself in glorious technicolour enjoying the very thing that you don't normally enjoy, feeling deep pleasure and excitement for the task in hand. Now open your eyes. If you continued to do that exercise regularly, several times a day, you would find those excited feelings entering your mind and body when you come into contact with your given situation. Perhaps you will even start eating vegetables with great excitement! So, emotions can also be linked to behaviour.

However, not all associations are good. The other side of this coin is that behavioural psychologists believe that humans will go to enormous lengths to avoid what gives them pain or displeasure. If you see someone coming who you would rather not deal with, you will go to any length to avoid them. This is called our natural defence mechanism. We seek to avoid pain or discomfort in most circumstances, and it is the rational or irrational fear of that being present that causes us to avoid some serious communications.

For example, Naomi is an aggressive; Peter is shy. You have worked with both of them in the past. Peter is so scared of Naomi performing one of her outbursts that he decides to stay away from her altogether, just in case. Naomi is chosen to upgrade her job to a more senior position, dealing with computer software (her strong subject) and the organisation needs to create another senior manager post to handle the hardware side of the same project. Peter would be ideal for this because he is very knowledgeable about computer hardware but his enjoyment for this activity (the pleasure) is overshadowed by his inability to handle Naomi (the pain). Unless he develops an effective way of working with Naomi that results in him feeling in control of each of her aggressive moods (or he is able to deflate them) the pain will always be stronger than the pleasure. Peter needs more balance in his feelings, and that is where you, as a fellow colleague, have been asked to support and help.

Naomi may not like it but she needs to accept that her style of working may work well for her but not for other people. (Obviously this should have been addressed some time ago, but some people are resistant to tackling aggressive characters.) You decide to speak to Naomi but she is resistant to changing her style of communication because – and here is the crunch – she wants the project to go well. She cannot see that her behaviour is having a negative impact at all. She confesses that she sees this opportunity as a chance to show senior managers what she is capable of, and is looking for a permanent promotion. She is desperate for Peter to work alongside her to make that happen, as he is by far the most knowledgeable member of staff when it comes to computer hardware. To enable this to happen, Peter needs Naomi to change. There is the conundrum – they both need to make some changes to enable the project to go ahead but neither of them feel it is really necessary. Naomi feels that her aggression will secure a successful project and that Peter should learn to live with it. Peter refuses to work with her until she agrees to modify her behaviour.

In this scenario, Peter actually holds all the cards because Naomi needs him to work on the project. With your help, Peter is therefore able to tap into Naomi's 'what's in it for me?' (or WIIFM) driver. For the outcome to be successful the WIIFM driver has to be stronger than any other to enforce change. Put simply, if there is nothing positive or rewarding for the individual in effecting that change, they may choose not to do it – and, in Naomi's case, if the results she achieves are so much better by using her aggression, she will not see why she should change. It is therefore down to you and Peter to use Naomi's WIIFM driver to demonstrate that she does indeed need him to pull this project off and therefore she needs to temper her behaviour accordingly.

Trying to identify each person's WIIFM drive can be very helpful, and you can do this subtly by asking them over a break time coffee, 'The project you are working on seems to be going very well, what personal satisfaction do you get from it?' or 'That looks good, how is this work going to help you in your career?' Sit back and see what unfolds. Their responses may surprise you.

Communicating pressure points at your level

There may be many times when you need to communicate pressure points and concerns at your level to other colleagues. It is not always acceptable to say that you feel stressed as that can be perceived as a weakness in some organisations. Therefore, before you cry on a colleague's shoulder in the rest room, think through a few options.

Let's get one aspect out of the way: it is all right to express your emotions. In fact, the people who are able to use their emotions to great effect have higher levels of emotional intelligence. Emotional intelligence is a concept made popular by Daniel Goleman in his book of the same title. In this he identified five main areas of emotional intelligence:

- Self awareness – knowing your own internal preferences and feelings.
- Self-regulation – managing those internal preferences and feelings.
- Motivation – emotional tendencies that guide or facilitate goals.
- Empathy – awareness of the feeling of others
- Social skills – the ability to induce a desirable response in others.

For example, one of the key factors required in business today is resilience. This is the need to be able to recover quickly from setbacks. Being able to reframe situations and think clearly in a difficult situation is another aspect of emotional intelligence. Resilience links directly with emotional intelligence as it taps into several of Goleman's key areas above.

However, demonstrating your emotional intelligence to others does not mean sobbing openly at the first sign of trouble. Emotions need to be kept in some form of balance to be considered genuine. It must also be expected that how you operate emotionally will be judged by others. Now, before you shy away from this and say, 'Then I won't show any emotions', I have to tell you that even no emotional response is an emotional response. In other words, when you choose to demonstrate no emotion you are in danger of depicting yourself as emotionally cold or aloof and uncaring. There is no getting away from it, in every activity, your emotional response is there for everyone to judge.

Now the second point. You must never forget that, however helpful you are to each other, there will always be professional tensions between colleagues. Like siblings who vie for the attention of their parents and crave their approbation, this tension may also be very real across colleague relationships. Not everyone would directly stab a colleague in the back, but there are more subtle ways of gaining one-upmanship, such as by offering faint praise, and so you need to be on your guard.

When going to colleagues is not always possible because of their other vested interests, then you need another outlet for gaining a sympathetic ear. A place where you can discuss your problems, and gain help with challenging questions. A safe wall to bounce ideas off can be crucial as there will be many occasions when you are simply too close to the problem to see the answer. In these instances, rather than go to a colleague, ask your manager about arranging for a mentor.

Mentors are often sounding boards, and can be either people from inside or outside the organisation. They tend to work specifically with work problems and processes (such as how to manage change at work) and bring a great deal of their own experience into the discussion. For this reason, mentors are often selected for their seniority of position, their high level of knowledge and their personal experience. Having a mentor can be hugely productive, for example, who else could you talk to confidentially if you were thinking of making changes at work, or with your team? And wouldn't it be helpful to talk through the process with someone who can give the short-cut to all the things you need to think about and who you can trust to give you good quality advice? Having access to a mentor can also increase self confidence. Mentors give instant feedback and don't hold back when it is time to tell someone that they have made a great decision or handled something particularly well. Mentors can also provide advice on personal development, a factor that often gets forgotten in the turbulent world of work.

Finding commonalities and links

When dealing with other people at our own level, we need to communicate effectively and also build a sufficiently robust relationship that enables us to work together on joint projects. We do not need to be friends but it helps if, as mentioned above, we are not adversaries either. The shortest route to building quick relationships is through the identification of commonalities and links.

Sounds like it should be easy? Well, for most people it's not. Like the saying, 'birds of a feather flock together', like it or not, we are all prejudiced. We do not necessarily mix easily with people we do not know and naturally congregate into groups of people who fit our 'people like me' criteria. If you were to walk into a conference or public area and needed to network, you would immediately be trying to identify someone who fitted into your 'people like me' framework. Finding that person would immediately be followed by a verbal exchange where you tried to find out something you have in common, however tenuous the link. You may even then try to verbalise this to someone else, to give it credibility, for example, 'Jim, meet Tim. He used to work in the city just like us.'

We look for links (possibly facts) that provide us with anchors, for example, 'Pete was born in Ireland too', or common experiences such as 'Jan also went to a grammar school'. This is why reunions are more successful in creating bonds than casual meetings – you have all shared the same experience, and that gets the conversational ball rolling. We naturally find it hard to link with people with whom we have nothing in common as there is no basis for any discussion, and no comparators against which to judge their perception of any new experiences. For example, if you know someone is from the same organisation as you, you will be able to make a broad assumption that they feel similarly to yourself and have the same perceptions about common things such as how everyone feels about the last CEO. This can, of course, go horribly wrong and you may make an assumption as to their feelings that is entirely incorrect.

Finding legitimate commonalities and links is therefore very important. It makes us feel less isolated, more in touch with others, and is a boon for those who like to network. If you are ever at a networking event or need to make a connection with someone fast – perhaps you will soon be working together – the fastest way to success is to find that link, and use it to build a bridge of understanding between you both.

Exercise

Next time you need to meet new colleagues or work with someone on a project, find out as much as you can about them first and make the connections. It is the fastest way of building relationships, and culturing relationships is the fastest way to networking and gaining a wide span of colleagues.

Being forgiving

Work colleagues will fall out. You may be competing for the same goal or cross each other over your work. Stress and pressure impact on how we interact with each other and the stage is set for miscommunication to occur. Metaphorical daggers are drawn and a stand-off seems inevitable. How can you ever work with this person again? How can you ever forgive their actions or words? When all is said and done, one of the biggest human skills is that of forgiveness. It is another feature that sets us apart from animals, and makes us far more sophisticated. Forgiveness is also a very personal judgement on a situation, and although those who forgive openly often appear to have the moral high ground, it has to come from the heart for it to be genuine.

We all judge other people all the time, and the only template we have available that we truly know well is ourselves. For this reason we often compare others to ourselves and their acts to those we would undertake. How many times have you heard people say with indignation, 'I wouldn't do that', even though what the person concerned is doing is not really wrong? Perhaps they have a different way of doing things or way of acting, but by retorting, 'I wouldn't do that', they are not just responding to the act itself, they are putting a value judgement on it, and this value judgement is usually 'I'm right and you are wrong'. The psychologist, Berne, expressed it slightly differently in his work on Transactional Analysis. He talked about four states:

1. I'm OK, you're not OK (as mentioned above)
2. I'm not OK, but you're OK
3. I'm not OK, you're not OK
4. I'm OK, you're OK

Let's look at these in more detail:

I'm OK, you're not OK – This is not a healthy state because it is passing judgement on the other person and finding them lacking. It shows an implied superiority, putting yourself above the other individual, and is no basis for mutual discussions at the same level.

I'm not OK, but you're OK – This demonstrates an empowering of the other person, detrimental to yourself. It demonstrates a lack of inner certainty and passivity – confident and assertive people do not provide other people with the ammunition to shoot them down!

I'm not OK, you're not OK – A very sad position where the individual cannot see good in themselves or others. They may be depressed or perhaps disenchanted, but whatever is the cause of this, it is not a healthy place to be.

I'm OK, you're OK – This is the healthiest state of all. It demonstrates balance and an acknowledgement of equality, in addition to mutual respect. We are both OK, we might have different ideas and opinions but they are both valid. It is in this state that we are able to forgive.

Now let us look at forgiveness in relation to ourselves and others. Whereas we might suggest that one person forgives another, it is a personal state that the individual either wishes to happen or not to happen. No amount of you saying that I should forgive someone will make it come about until I decide to feel it in my heart and let the bad feelings go. It takes so much more energy to hold a grudge than to let it go, feel happy and accept the situation – but that decision to let negative feelings go must come from the individual concerned. Therefore breaking out of a cycle of dislike and bad feeling can give you the energy to fight other more important battles elsewhere. Letting go can be cathartic and cleansing; some people can dislike another colleague for years and they can't even remember how it all started. Ultimately they are only damaging themselves and bizarrely, there are occasions when the other person does not even know about it.

It is not always possible to forgive but where you can, you should, if only for your own health and wellbeing. We all walk the earth together and need to rely on each other from time to time. When something negative happens with a colleague, consider:

- You may be angry but does your level of wrath justify the incident?
- How would it sound if you described the incident to someone else? Would it sound foolish?
- If someone were describing the situation to you, what would you recommend?
- How would you feel if that person was involved in a tragic accident on the way home from work that night?
- How would you feel if that person were suddenly promoted into the position of your boss?
- Do you honestly feel that continuing this feud is productive?
- Be honest, do you secretly gain pleasure from this?

It may be that you are holding on to this hurt because you gain from it in some way. Maintaining bad feelings about colleagues is common, albeit rarely productive. Be the first to show that you can forgive incidents and your relationships will flourish in the future.

Case study 3

Colin Cool and Simon Snide both work for B.B. Bothers, an IT systems company. They have both come into the organisation through a graduate scheme and have joined direct from university. They both have similar degrees and the only difference between them is their attitude to work and to other staff.

Colin Cool decides that work is very important to him and that he would very much like to move up in the organisation. He decides that he will be supportive of others who also want to get on, but will remain one step ahead by using his own background and knowledge to solve problems. He will also tap into the knowledge and expertise of others and use their help appropriately, giving due credit for results. He will ask HR for a mentor in senior management and will openly learn from his mistakes.

Simon Snide also decides that work is very important to him and that he would very much like to move up in the organisation. However, he decides that he needs to demonstrate his superiority over colleagues by achieving his targets at any cost (including putting them down at every turn). He will also take out the opposition (Colin) by making snide comments about him to senior managers, and will fire-fight problems by, in some cases, starting the fire first, before racing in to put it out.

Colin and Simon have been asked to work on a project together and Simon has decided that there can be only one 'winner' – the person who comes out looking good – and it must be him. Colin tries to be inclusive but Simon takes work away and does not share the results with Colin. Simon also finds out that Colin goes dancing one night per week and takes great joy in ridiculing him to the other project staff, behind his back.

What do you think Colin should do?

Conclusion

The colleague relationship is full of flex and change. You could join the organisation and be put in a group of colleagues, perhaps on a graduate scheme, at the same level, and three years later some will have progressed and others will not. Professional colleagues are not always colleagues in the truest sense. Any friendship will be sorely tested through time and actions. Although no one should ever refrain from workplace friendships, it is foolish to ignore the dynamics that go on at collegial level, and how the seductive search for power often comes at the cost of someone else's fall.

Understanding the problems that can surround workplace colleague relationships will ensure that you consider every aspect and thereby enjoy healthier and more realistic relationships with your fellow workers.

INSTANT TIP

Find out the level of interaction you need to have with work colleagues and assess not only your liking for them, but also take a measure of your respect in their ability. You may have difficult colleagues who require a high level of understanding but the quality of their work means that the investment in time is well worth it.

06

Difficult customers – how do I deal with them?

All businesses need customers. Somebody somewhere has to buy something, whether that be tangible goods and products or services. The customer is immensely important to the transaction and in large organisations, where people deal only with numbers, it may seem that no one actually sees the customer – but that does not mean that they are not there. Businesses need customers to operate and whatever your role, you need to be aware of their impact. Customer fickleness is also legendary and a lack of awareness of how your customers think, together with future trends, could lead you to be seriously out of step.

The customer relationship, however, does not have to be one-sided. Customers can be rude, difficult and downright annoying but you both need each other – or do you? If you are having serious problems with a customer, you might be tempted to think about the balance to which you both contribute to the transaction, and let a lower payback go.

For example, a customer who buys TVs in blocks of 50 or more for the rooms in his chain of hotels has a problem that needs resolving. You will surely be very keen to help him out as you know for sure he will be back again if you can assure him of a swift resolution. But what about the lady who buys one TV and has a problem? Do you treat her the same or do you think, 'Well she is a small spender, so let her complain, I don't have to deal with it if I don't want to.' Let's see what happens when we ignore her and also fail to be aware of the multiplier effect.

The Accumulator Effect

Now let us assume this TV was priced at £200, and you told the customer that you were not going to deal with the problem.

The lady in the example above goes to a family dinner that night with four other people who were naturally enquiring about her day. Of course, she tells them about her problem, warning them away from ever doing business with you. Those four people represent 4 × £200 = £800 in possible lost revenue.

Now imagine that the following day, they each tell another four people about their relative's problem, which would represent 16 × £200 = £3200 of possible lost revenue. So far, that is £4000 of possible lost revenue from not dealing with one person effectively.

I know what you are thinking, that probably those people were not all going to buy a £200 TV in the near future. Well, maybe some of them were, and maybe some were going to spend more – in fact it is likely that, were any of these people to buy a TV at all in the future, they would not now 'risk' buying from you, after all, there are so many other places to choose from. It is also highly likely that they would pass this story on to many more people than in the example – the story might even make it into the local papers!

The accumulator effect can be hugely damaging – if you are still not convinced consider the case of a certain famous jewellers and how their business all but disappeared overnight following flippant comments by one of the directors, regarding the quality of their goods, on national television.

There is also the issue of the internal customer. When organisations depend on internal divisions to provide a service to each other, this necessarily creates the concept of internal customisation. For example, when the sales team need to send their orders to the finance department so that they can raise invoices, this action then triggers the manufacturing team to create the products. This creates a web of internal services. If those departmental services are not treating each other as official customers, communication and turn around of information could become sluggish with the result that process times become longer and mistakes are made. By taking the view that everyone is the customer of someone else – even within the business – processes can become more streamlined and there is more of a sense of everyone contributing towards the whole.

Being prompt in identifying the real issues

If you are a customer of goods or services that do not meet your personal idea of quality, what do you do? You would probably think that you ought to complain or get your feelings across to someone because you want something done about the situation. You may also think that perhaps someone should be responsible for this error. The key point here is that you would want someone to:

- acknowledge the situation, and then hopefully
- take some form of action.

This is where so many people go wrong in customer care. The first step can take but a few minutes but the second step – the action – may take longer. However, what often happens is that in taking time to consider what the second step may be, who you should speak to, or what recompense is ever offered, the first step is put on hold. The result of this is that the customer is left not knowing whether their original complaint has been received, acknowledged or ignored. It is this total lack of information that makes them even more angry. The next time they phone up – Pow! – you really are likely to feel the full force of their anger, which now may be totally out of proportion to the situation.

To prevent this outburst it is important that we rethink steps one and two again. An initial fast and efficient way of dealing with customer issues can prevent many long-term problems. When dealing with customer issues at the initial stage the most important aspects are being able to:

- hear the problem
- take effective notes
- acknowledge the feelings behind the problem
- undertake some form of action
- follow through.

Let's just look at that in more detail.

Hear the problem

This means actually paying close attention to what the issue is. When a customer describes a problem to you they may start in a number of places. They may start at the main issue, perhaps a malfunction of a product, or by describing how the product was bought, where it was bought from, how annoyed they feel, or even with a description of their holiday, detailing why they bought the product! What is essential is that you listen carefully and extract the details while homing in on the real issue under dispute. Also try to ascertain what the customer actually wants as recompense. It is helpful to know whether someone complaining about a malfunctioning camera is asking for a repair, a replacement, or recompense for the whole wedding that was ruined due to the lack of photographs.

Take effective notes

These will help you, or whoever is dealing with the problem, later on. When taking details it helps to remember Kipling's 'Six Honest Serving Men':

I know six honest serving men
(They taught me all I knew)
Their names are What and Why and When
And How and Where and Who.

In essence:

- What is the situation?
- Where did it happen (or where is the item)?
- Why did this happen or come about?
- How did it happen?
- When did it happen?
- To whom did it happen?

Acknowledge the feelings behind the problem

The problem is not the only problem, when it comes to customer care. The other issue is how the customer is feeling about the situation. Two customers may react totally differently to a similar situation. For one, a broken product is a mere inconvenience and, for another, the end of the world. Never be judgemental, the problem is as the customer sees it, and what they want more than anything is their feelings acknowledged. You must never admit fault, after all you have not undertaken an investigation yet, but you can acknowledge how the customer must be feeling. Saying, 'I can understand how this situation must have distressed you', demonstrates concern, but without ascribing blame to either side.

Undertake some form of action

This is not the final action or outcome, this is something you can do NOW to help this person. Summarise the situation as you now understand it, tell the customer that you have made notes, who they will be passed on to, and when they can expect to be contacted and the method. Immediately treat this as urgent to contain the problem as being the initial problem and not some escalated version of the situation, and take the next step as necessary, whether that be seeking help or passing it on to another relevant person. One simple action you can do immediately is to write to the customer expressing your concern at their displeasure, and detailing how their complaint will be handled, including names and timescales. An example letter is shown in Figure 6.1.

Morris Fosbrooks Ltd
Basingstoke
BS17 8JJ

Mrs Holmes
Bankside
Little Hempstead
Hampshire
SO9 6PN

{date}
{reference number}

Dear Mrs Holmes

Thank you for your phone call. I am so sorry that you appear to be having problems with our new Superscreen product. I can assure you that this is very unusual and we are currently engaged in finding a way in which we can help you.

Your complaint is being handled by Sandra Stokes, the manager of the production team. Sandra will be carrying out an investigation and will contact you by phone and letter within the next ten days.

If in the meantime you would like to check progress at any time during the process, please ring Sandra on XXXX XXXXX.

Yours faithfully

Peter Truly
Customer Care Manager

Figure 6.1: An example letter

Follow through

Nothing will annoy a customer more than if promises are not held. This will add even more fire to their already burning anger and, for many, a lack of follow through will be the final straw. They will not do business with you again. Keep them informed and updated on every stage of the process, and there is a good chance you will win them back.

It is unrealistic to believe that there will not be some faults with all the products and services that we use in our lifetime, but the way in which these are handled lead either to customers turning their backs or to customer loyalty.

Following the above complaint, there needs to be an investigation. This may be undertaken by yourself or a customer care specialist. An investigation is usually conducted by someone of management grade, as they may very possibly need to report the outcome to the Board. Repeated complaints often result in a change of design, system or process, and that may be a Board decision. Whatever the outcome, a list of customer complaints must always be kept and recorded so that problems can be tracked, with a view to them being eradicated.

Is the problem situational or personal?

However, what happens when the problem is not about a product but a person? This adds a new dimension to dealing with the issue at large. It may be that the customer is complaining about a sales assistant, someone on the telephone, the person who is handling their complaint, or possibly even yourself. They may have seen the person, perhaps in the case of a shop or a sales assistant, or they may never have met them and dealt only with them by mail, phone or e-mail.

The first thing to try to ascertain is whether it is the person they are actually complaining about. What may initially appear to be a complaint about a person may actually be a veiled complaint about the system. The customer may just not like what they have heard (the message) and decide to address this with an assault on the messenger. In a situation where there is a complaint about a person, it is important then, to separate:

- the message given
- the way in which it was delivered
- the person who delivered the message.

The message given

This could be that your organisation's procedures do not marry up with the expectations of the customer. For example, you may have a policy that any complaint that is received outside of the warranty period is not to be dealt with. If this is the case, a complaint against a customer telephone officer may be an underlying annoyance about your policy rather than the person themselves.

The way in which it was delivered

All staff dealing with customer complaints should undergo some form of customer care training. There are different ways of conveying a message and the tone and phrase in which a message is given can have a great effect on how it is received. Whereas it is not always essential for an organisation to maintain a full customer care team, it might be worth all staff attending customer care training to ensure they deliver a consistent message and deal with all complaints in the same manner.

The person who delivered the message

There may be occasions when the complaint does come down to the individual. Given that we have already mentioned the problems caused by leaving customers hanging on, not following procedures, or not having any respect for the customer at all, any of this may point to poor business behaviour. If you find this to be the problem, you will need to speak with the individual and decide the next course of action. In the short term, and to help the customer, it would be pertinent to appoint another person to deal with the original complaint, or deal with it yourself. In the longer term you have a performance issue that you now need to address with the staff member, and this may mean you liaising with another manager if they are not in your department or team.

When following up a customer difficulty about a person, if they are found to be at fault, it becomes a management issue as to how it should be addressed. There are a number of supportive measures, such as training, mentoring, work shadowing, or there is the option to distance them from customer contact. In extreme circumstances, and with the weight of other evidence, this may even result in them having to leave the organisation.

It is for this very reason that so many organisations either have their own customer contact line (to ensure customers are dealt with by experienced professionals in a consistent way) or buy into a commercial customer care centre. If an organisation has its own customer care officer or manager, problems can be routed through to one person and a co-ordinated approach taken, rather than being handled by anyone who happens to pick up the phone. On the other hand, commercial centres offer customer care staff for a number of organisations. The benefit of using this type of centre is that all staff are fully trained in dealing with customer care issues and at the end of the phone they are relatively anonymous. As they are handling complaints from a range of organisations, and charge per operation, they can be a much cheaper option than employing a customer care officer who may just be sitting around, waiting.

There is the added advantage that often their calls are recorded and therefore any complaints regarding how a customer is treated can be re-run and assessed.

Not everyone is suited to handling customer care issues. It requires an upbeat, positive 'can do' approach that at the same time is grounded by strong listening and empathic skills. No customer wants to be met by a jolly clown who tells them that 'everything will be just fine', but they won't want to deal with a 'Negative Nigel' either. The approach your department takes to customer care should be embedded in your business plan, and be evident in every way you interact with both internal and external customers. A total customer care approach by the whole team will reduce customer complaints over a period of time and will soon become 'the way things are done around here'.

Exercise

Who is dealing with customer care in your organisation? Is there any need for you to be involved in any part of the process? Would that include exposure to the customer? Do you need some specialist training for this role? How clued up are your staff about external and internal customer care issues, and how to route a complaint? Are they clear about the role of the customer in running your department's business?

Are there things you can put right?

When it comes to dealing with difficult customers, you need to be very sure of your mandate. What exactly can you offer customers and what is out of bounds? For example, you may be able to offer them money in compensation, but it might have to come directly out of your own budget! Or perhaps every compensation, however small, has to be discussed and signed off by senior management. In other words, you need to be clear about the parameters surrounding any offers you can make. Initially there are a number of things you may be able to do such as write to a complainant or speak to them, offering them your name as a management level contact and offering reassurance. Do not think that these things matter less than remuneration, they are equally as important. From there on you will need to undertake either an investigation or package of remuneration in accordance with your company policy.

In some organisations, and many parts of local government, monetary awards to external customers are certainly discouraged. In the retail sector vouchers are often given, ensuring that the customer has to come back to spend them, and hopefully has a better experience next time. It is certainly worth finding out what the difficult customer thinks is sufficient recompense. If they are making themselves difficult because they want a monetary payout and that is not your policy, it is worth stating that upfront, as that may well end the situation.

Exercise

Find out how your organisation typically deals with customers. What is their policy/approach? What is your mandate to offer platitudes or deal direct with customers?

Customer Relationship Management (CRM) is an approach whereby you actively reach out to customers and try to build a relationship with them. The theory is that if you are in a relationship with your customers they are more likely to engage with you and work through any problems. Through this approach you can also contact your customers to enable their opinions to shape your business and then offer them new products. This approach has been embraced by industries such as personal banking, but can easily be adapted for most businesses.

What are your grounds for negotiation?

So, you have established that your customer has some grounds for complaint but you have not agreed to the extent of the problem or any further action. At the moment the customer is angry. How can you turn this situation around? Well, you could move immediately to settlement of the issue (in whatever way you decide), but then you lose a big opportunity to engage with the customer and perhaps win back their trust and future business. In this situation you are in a position to negotiate, and the negotiation is again not just about the terms of settlement but about engaging the customer and hopefully winning them over for the future.

There are four stages to negotiation:

- **Preparation** – find out all you can about the situation, how long it has been going on for, what has been written/said, this customer's track record, what they want to achieve.
- **Discuss** – other staff may have been involved in this situation before you stepped in. Find out from anyone who has dealt with this customer before, what their likely response will be. If you need to, agree an approach with another manager.
- **Propose** – decide either independently or with your organisation what the parameters of any award may be (at this stage there may be minimum and maximum amounts).
- **Bargain** – handle the negotiation with the customer, aiming for a win–win situation if possible.

In any situation, there are four possible outcomes from a negotiation:

- **Win–lose** – this is where you win on the negotiation but at the expense of the other person. For example, 'No we will not offer you anything and suggest you shop elsewhere in the future.'
- **Lose–win** – this is where you lose but the customer wins. For example, 'I am sorry that the spillage spoilt your clothes. We will pay for the dry cleaning bill and also offer you a year's free dining at any of our restaurants.'
- **Lose–lose** – in this outcome you are both losers. For example, 'I will replace everything at my own personal cost and I fully understand that you don't want to shop here again.'
- **Win–win** – this is the ideal outcome, where you both get something out of the negotiation, for example, 'We will replace the product, including postage, and send you a voucher for 10 per cent discount on your next purchase. We are sorry that this mistake has happened and hope that you will remain a good customer of Busy PCs.'

In the win–win situation you will see that the customer achieved their result – a speedy resolution – and also came away with a voucher, which has cost Busy PCs very little in actual money as the discount will come off their mark-up. The customer feels they have something extra and the voucher means that they are more inclined to go back there in the future, if only to browse what to possibly spend it on.

When trying to reach a win–win situation with a difficult customer:

ALWAYS

Respect people as individuals and don't pull rank otherwise you will inflame the situation further.

Be honest.

Acknowledge that your viewpoint may be different and acknowledge that you understand the other's point of view.

Make the effort to explore all the possibilities that could lead to everyone gaining swift resolution from the situation.

NEVER

Lie, bluster or lose your temper.

Judge, criticise or nit-pick.

Jump to conclusions.

Be limiting – think of all possibilities.

Withhold necessary information.

Use unethical tactics to ensure you win.

A successful negotiation can actually win you customer support in the long run and once again who will these one-time difficult people tell? Other people, of course, and you will have turned a negative customer situation into a positive one.

Case study 4

Peter Smith is a constant complainer. He buys from your business regularly and does not comment at the time but regularly phones up to complain afterwards. His complaints are petty but he returns the goods in the same condition in which they were sold and usually has his money returned or a replacement. Your company has a good returns policy but it is just his constant time-wasting that is the problem. Every time you hear the phone ring, you assume it is him yet again and your heart sinks – there goes another hour of your time wasted in sorting this situation out again.

You have established that he is a regular returning customer and have looked at the figures. Peter Smith retains more than he returns and if it were not for those returns, he would be considered a most valuable customer. What is the problem and what options do you have?

Case study 5

Patsy works in the payment section. She has been there one year but is terribly slow at processing your customers' payments. The processing of the payment triggers the goods to be packaged before being passed to the customer. Patsy's slowness therefore impacts on the whole process and the customers ring you when they don't receive their goods in the time advised by the sales team. You are the manager that deals with customer care and therefore not Patsy's line manager. What should you do about this?

Conclusion

When you are dealing with difficult customers you need to decide initially whether there is a case for their annoyance. If there is, then the fault lies with your organisation and you need to speak with senior management about improving your quality and systems. If it really is the customer who is difficult, consider first how much their business is worth to you, and whether, rather than pushing them away, you should really be involving them more.

There is never a need to tolerate abuse. Most companies will have policies regarding this but, if after warning the customer that you will not tolerate that type of behaviour, they continue you should terminate any conversation or phone call. Abuse is not an effective form of communication and therefore will never lead to a satisfactory resolution.

INSTANT TIP

Clients and customers hold the key to business but they are not free to treat you disrespectfully. Ensure your organisation has clear guidelines for handling clients and customers, and put them into practice.

07

Difficult suppliers – how should I deal with them?

Suppliers do not just supply products or materials, they are also all your consultants, trainers, advisers, professional bodies – in fact anyone who provides you with information, goods and services. When a supplier falters in their provision there are a number of options available to you and it is quite clear that, if the goods and services are not being provided, you must either find another way of obtaining them – or redesigning your processes so that you no longer need them. But what if the supplier is just being difficult? What happens if they withhold payment, start to impose new penalties in contracts that are not beneficial to you, or start to provide for a competitor? Where do you stand then and how do you deal with them?

Let's look at the background to this. The supply and demand chain is a fine balance between running a successful business and not having the materials to work with. It is rather like a web where everyone has their part. One tear in that web can affect the whole structure and although it may not bring it down completely, it becomes more fragile and unbalanced until the tear is repaired again. This fragility helps no one and companies can be brought down by relatively minor 'tears' to their web. For example, news may leak of a problem (perhaps a problem with material supply) and that could, in turn, lead to downturn in consumer confidence, that results in a reduction in the share price. A shortage in the supply of grain will cause food prices to soar and can trigger panic buying and stock storage. This is no help to the overall economy as, like a river, it needs to run freely.

When you have a healthy relationship between suppliers and buyers, you work not only in your own interest but also in each other's interest because it helps no one if one of you should fail. Many companies have helped their suppliers, perhaps by giving them more favourable terms or offering loans, because it is in their interest to ensure that everyone stays commercially viable. For this reason it is not uncommon for companies to even buy out their supplier if the supplier gets into financial difficulties. Businesses depend on other businesses for their survival and the relationship between them is a finely balanced one.

Getting it in perspective

Problems with suppliers can become very emotional and therefore it is a good idea to put the whole situation into perspective before rushing in with an ill-judged solution. Decisions made on the hoof often cause other problems later on. For example, if caught out with a sudden price rise from the supplier you may be tempted to immediately accept their new prices, just to get the order delivered – but what will that do for your business long term? You may not be able to pass the increase on to the customer, and therefore make very little profit. This would not be sustainable in the long run, but if you have agreed to the new price now, is it giving the message that you always will? Will that ruin your negotiating stance? Situations like this need to be thought through carefully before action takes place, no matter what the hurry is at the time. Decisions usually have ramifications for the business elsewhere in the chain.

Let's look at a more analytical or process approach. You are having a problem with one of your suppliers:

1. Firstly, is this a situation you (or your organisation) has caused? This initial question is important not just to judge who is the aggrieved party, but if it is something you have caused, you may be able to put things right again. For example, you may have changed your payment dates and that now makes it impossible for your supplier to buy their raw material in time to produce their order for you. If that is the case, then you may be able to move it back to the original dates again. If so, problem solved!

2. Secondly, is this a one-off problem, or an ongoing one? You need to know whether you are dealing with a 'for now' situation or one that will keep recurring. For a one-off situation or problem you might put in emergency measures or even pay a little more to get you out of a fix but this is not sustainable. For example, the guy who supplies your web-presence (looking after your website and online advertising) breaks his arm in an accident. You are desperate to get a new offer out to your internet customers and so you start to look at who else could do it. All other suppliers of this service want to charge you at least twice the cost because you are not offering a long-term contract, but you may reason that this is a one-off situation, and as your original guy will be back at work as soon as he can be, you will pay and take the hit of the extra costs (and appreciate him more in the future)! In other words, it is worth throwing some money at this one because the problem is a short-term one.

3. Thirdly, in which part of your business is the problem? Not all areas of your business are equal. Some products or services are more key to business success than others, some yield more profit, and this may affect how you react to a supplier problem. For example, if an area is key to your business success you will view any supplier problem as having critical effect, whereas if the business area has much less impact on bottom-line performance, you may decide to deal with the problem differently. To compare your areas of work or products and find out which ones are crucial it is useful to measure them against the Boston Consulting Group Approach (see Figure 7.1).

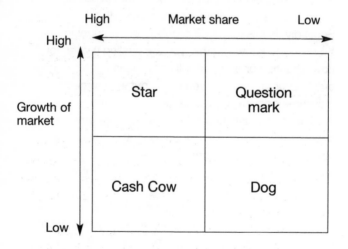

Figure 7.1: The Boston Matrix

The Boston Consulting Group Approach uses four segments or categories of service/product as rated against the market growth rate and the relative market share (as shown in Figure 7.1).

- **Star products/services are those that are high-growth, high-share.** They often need heavy investment to finance their rapid growth. Eventually their growth will slow down and they will turn into Cash Cows. Dealing with a problem supplier in this segment can be very tricky. You are on a roll and you want to generate as much from Star products/services as possible, so it might be worth paying more to your supplier or finding another immediately, whatever the cost.

- **Cash Cows are low-growth, high-share. They are established and successful.** They need less investment and produce a lot of cash for the business. They are often used to pay the bills and fund research and development in other parts of the business. You need Cash Cows because they keep on generating income (for an example, think of many of the traditional sweets that have been on the market for over 40 years and need no advertising). You will have to balance out a problem supplier here – you are likely to be in long-term relationships with suppliers and it is in both your interests to ensure it continues, so there needs to be a good analysis. Depending on the product/service you may be able to hang out for some time, but the other thing to remember here is that Cash Cows are just that, they generate a lot of money and while there is a problem, it halts the flow of money coming into the business.

- **Question marks are low-share, in a high-growth market.** They require a lot of cash or input to hold their share, let alone increase it. Some of these may turn into Stars but others may need phasing out. These are tricky. If they are not yet Stars then I would suggest that if you have a problem with a supplier here, you stop and try to work something out. They are not generating much capital and therefore you need not be held ransom by the supplier.

- **Dogs are low-share, low-growth.** They may be self-
  funding but never promise to be great cash generators.
  Any problems with suppliers here and you may just let the
  whole thing drop, or freeze the project until things have
  been sorted out. You certainly don't need hassle in this
  segment as the return is not worth the effort.

Now that you have these three pieces of analytical information, you
should be more able to react in an appropriate manner based on
solid information rather than gut feelings and panic. If it is to be the
end of the relationship, at least it will be based on logical thinking
and some solid facts, rather than gut instinct clouded by emotion.

Looking at your previous relationship

Thousands of new businesses open up worldwide every year. If you
look to the international market the number is mind boggling – and
they are all after your business. Some are willing to offer generous
incentives to new customers, and others (such as fuel companies)
are even willing to handle the switch-over for you. If you have been
dealing with the same supplier for years because it is either too
difficult to change or you think no one else out there offers the
same, it is time to look again.

Every so often it pays to undertake a proper supplier analysis.
This means looking not only at your suppliers but who else is out
there and what would be the implications of changing supplier.
Questions you need to ask are:

- **Who are your suppliers?** Think about your business as a
  whole. Who supplies everything from the staples to the
  key components? Who provides you with temporary staff?

Who supplies your stationery? How long have you been trading with them, and what is their track record? Are you buying from two suppliers where one could suffice (and you may be able to negotiate a greater discount)? Also note how you access your supplies. You may pay more to a local supplier but save on transportation or postage costs.

● **Who else is out there?** Some items such as stationery have plentiful competition but others such as a factory floor sweeping machine will have very few. Although rare, in some instances your supplier may be the only one. Again, look at the geographical issue. Certain goods are cheaper to buy from different parts of the country, or even abroad, perhaps where wages are lower and housing costs less. The internet is a good place to start to find out who is offering what but also consider asking local Business Links and Chamber of Commerce and also consult trade directories.

● **What would be implications of change?** You need to think broadly on this one. Closing an account with a supplier in one department could cause another to lose their 'goodwill discount' because the supplier viewed the two accounts as the total commitment from your business. Business is more than money, and you run the risk of spoiling a helpful relationship, if you don't consider every implication. You need to see the bigger picture before you make such an important decision.

Now for the emotional angle. Be honest, over the past few years, has the relationship been good? What emotions are tied up in the relationship? Are the suppliers personal friends of yours or even family members? Do you have a reciprocal arrangement whereby your business helps them out? If you answered yes to any of these questions, you may find that it is not so easy to change because you have a psychological contract that is greater than just paper and ink. A psychological contract means that you have both accepted and bought into each other's businesses. The telltale signs are when your suppliers show a more than normal interest in your business and actively want to help you to grow so that your relationship can grow stronger. It is more than just wanting you to increase your order of supplies from them – they feel as involved in your business as in their own.

You have reached the point now where you know everything there is to know about your suppliers. Even if you decide to stick to your original supplier, you will have learnt so much more in readiness for any negotiation that may ensue, that you will be at an advantage. This exercise was focused on closely analysing your situation and not necessarily moving on from regular suppliers who may be difficult. You just need to know all the facts to make sure you begin to think about whether they are still the right suppliers for the future.

Are they right for your future?

Staying with the same supplier can be cosy, and what if they do become a little difficult? Your company has always traded with them, they don't mean it. There is no point looking around because they are all the same, aren't they? If we all thought like this no new businesses would ever get off the ground. All businesses have had to change over the years, and that includes giving you good customer service.

Customer service, as a phenomenon, came from the US and has now permeated most UK businesses. Today your business is not just who you are but also who you choose to do business with. The outcome of this is that everyone expects more from supplier relationships, and that suppliers will comply with the same network of values. However, the trends have not stopped there and there are a plethora of new values you need to consider when selecting a new supplier, or electing to remain with your exisiting supplier. The new kids on the block are: corporate responsibility, ethical trading, environmentally friendly (products and work ethic), flexibility, sustainability, IiP (Investors in People) and people care. In brief:

- **Corporate responsibility** This means an organisation demonstrating that it understands the responsibility it has for intruding into our lives. It could be that, for every 1000 boxes of paper that it sells, it will donate £100 to a neighbourhood project. Many companies now have their own charities that they openly support.
- **Ethical trading** This means that a company will only trade with companies that are ethical and have certain morals and values. The pay their staff a fair amount for the work they do and they contribute to local communities and society.
- **Environmentally friendly** This means that they use materials in all areas of their work that are just that – environmentally friendly. These materials are kinder to the environment and will largely be recyclable. They will deal with waste in the most environmentally safe way and will not discharge chemicals into rivers or throw computers onto landfill sites. Environmentally friendly will also cover any recycling policy the company may have.
- **Flexibility** How reactive can your business be? Building flexibility into a business means that it is more likely to weather any storm, and can be more reactive to change. They can also offer the customer so much more in the way of different options.
- **Sustainability** This refers to whether the business will be around in a few year's time. Businesses need to be able to survive in bad years as well as good, and if the company has thought about sustainability it will have built in a number of measures so that it can continue to survive

through the most difficult of times. Sustainability can be financial (as in salting away an amount of cash so that staff can be paid through lean times) or it can be built into products (such as the components being forever available from a recycled source).

● **IiP and people care** This is concerned with how staff are treated and kept informed. All staff should know how what they do in their jobs contributes to the bottom line of the business. It means keeping the information flow going so that ideas can be fed back, from all staff up to the business owner, and everyone feels engaged with the company and their job.

Why are we mentioning these new trends? Many suppliers are now being asked to demonstrate that they meet most of these criteria. It is no longer enough to buy from a supplier because they produce just what you want; they also need to demonstrate that they are able to supply these items from within a structure that is fair, ethical and environmentally sound. If a supplier is working with a local or government authority, they may also be asked to provide evidence of effective practice concerning diversity.

If you are working with suppliers, however effective they may be, that have not considered these aspects of their work they are seriously out of date. Considering that they will have been asked to complete these details by many other companies, if they appear vague I would be seriously concerned that they have a credible customer profile. The suppliers you use say something about your business and what you find acceptable, so ask the question and find out how compliant your supplier is.

Some organisations put suppliers into a position of bidding for the contract of supply. If that is the case, often these areas are used as a selection tool to enable someone to assess suitability. Who you work with says so much about your company that you need to make the selection wisely to avoid an unfortunate 'marriage'.

Building new supplier relationships that last

When you move into new relationships with suppliers there will always be the honeymoon period when you are both working to help each other. You are keen to get someone on board and get settled with a regular supplier, they are pleased to have a new customer and want to show their appreciation. It is a great time, but it won't necessarily last. It is not unusual to experience trouble at some point in any supplier/buyer relationship, but the degree to which that trouble rocks your foundations depends on how you have built your relationship.

Start by looking at any contracts and query those clauses that you do not understand, do not think are fair, or do not agree with. Contracts are negotiable: just because they say, 'payment in 10 days' does not mean that you cannot challenge this and negotiate an extension to something you may find more reasonable, but of course you need to do this at the beginning of the relationship. Your negotiating strength is severely diminished later on unless you are negotiating a huge order. If you agree to different terms and conditions, make sure this is also confirmed in writing. An e-mail is fine, but don't leave it to honour or memory – both can be severely tested!

As much as possible, deal in a transparent way. This means not hiding any aspects of the business from your supplier. Trust is essential in any relationship and if they suspect you are hiding something, you may find it difficult to recover. No one likes to feel that something is going on behind their backs or there is some ulterior motive, therefore keep transparency at the top of your agenda.

It is very difficult to start any relationship by assuming problems, but in the same way that a prenuptial agreement is becoming very fashionable, you need to think through what would happen if things went awry. It is very similar to producing a risk analysis that you might easily do on any project, but might not consider for any new supplier. Numerous services are outsourced today: what would you do if your IT service supplier was unable to provide a service one day because he had met an untimely accident? All suppliers are vulnerable and you might ask to see their emergency plan to ensure it meets your expectations. However, what about relationship problems? What if you have serious disagreements part way through a contract? The answer here is to make sure you have a mediation clause built into the contract. Mediation is where you come together, often with a third party, to sort out your problems and attempt resolution. It is a very positive process in that it assumes that problems will be solved and solutions found. If you think there may be problems in the future, rather than seeing the destruction of relations, and telling everyone, 'I could see that happening', put a clause in the contract to try to prevent it.

Build your supplier relationships on win–win wherever you can. Between you there is a great deal of power and opportunity. Some organisations openly recommend each other, and that is always good for business. Seize this opportunity to help each other and you could both be the better for it.

Case study 6

J. F. Loads is a small haulage company and you have worked with Mr Faulkner (the original owner) for some time. Mr Faulkner helped your business out in the early days by offering some lower cost transport when you did not have much money and it helped you to supply some customers that are key to your business's ongoing success, even though you know that J. F. Loads made very little on the deals. Mr Faulkner ran a tight, local business that dealt on a personal level with customers. As your business has grown, so has your relationship with J. F. Loads, and you have rarely had any cause for complaint – until now. Mr Faulkner is now about to retire and has brought in his son, Mark, fresh from business school, to run the business for him. You have met with Mark once and you were looking for reassurance that much of your relationship would not change. Mark, however, has other ideas. He is keen to tell you that not only does he know everything about the business (after all he grew up with it), but that he has great plans to expand nationally, 'Something that the old man seemed shy of.' You found him over-confident, with no real people skills and no experience of how your two businesses have worked together in the past. To make matters worse you have just received a contract from Mark informing you of their new terms of business, including (in the small print) veiled threats of court action for non-compliance. This all feels like a world away from the relationship you used to enjoy. What should you do?

Case study 7

You work for Castle Engineering Ltd, an established company of ten years. You used to source your screws and specialist bolts from Leonard Smith but after they were late with a couple of orders you blew your top at them, told them that the world is not that small that you cannot go elsewhere, and have been using another company that promised to undercut Leonard Smith's prices. You took them at their word and have now been ordering from Putnams for five months, although they have also let you down. Two orders have gone missing and the goods that arrived for another order were wrong. Putnams have now said that the lower price was for six months only and they will be raising their prices in four weeks. You did not check the small print and so now you are also trying to cover your tracks to your own boss. If he finds out you did not check all the paperwork before you switched contract, he will not be pleased with you. You are coming to realise that possibly you should have stayed with Leonard Smith, or at least read through the Putnams contract properly, but you let your emotions rule your head and now feel it would be impossible to go back. What should you do?

Conclusion

Dealing with suppliers is more than a daily transaction. There can be more than the contract on the table; there can also be a psychological contract in operation. At times you may feed off each other's customers and business, deals may be done and business shared, but the essential company–supplier relationship has to remain.

Where there are difficult relationships of any kind, this can add extra pressure with the opportunity for misunderstanding and the generation of problems. If you need to work together effectively consider a contract that specifies any nuances and stipulates how you will handle your relationship. For example, if the contract says you will pay your supplier in 30 days, you are in breach of it should you need to take a little longer. Similarly, if they have been contracted to offer you 20 days' consultancy each month, you would be short changed and feel duly aggrieved should you be told that the consultant is off sick and there is no one to cover for them. The contract may also include the manner in which you are both to conduct your business.

Using analysis you can start to calculate the real worth of your supplier and ascertain the cost to you of moving to someone new. You can then consider whether the suppliers you have really do help your business and add value to it, or devalue you by association. You then need to consider the relationship and whether this can be strengthened for the future. You could both be winners here as many companies run a tit-for-tat advertising campaign recommending each other. Finally, returning to the contract, it should button down most of the contentious issues that could not only cause you daily hassle but also long-term grief. The best way to treat suppliers is to work *with* them, and encourage them to approach you long before a small problem becomes a big one.

INSTANT TIP

Consider the supplier's long-term relationship with you and your organisation. Is the problem a one-off or a symptom of something far more serious on either side? If the former, consider ways of building the relationship; if the latter, consider whether other suppliers may offer a better relationship for the future.

08

How do I deal with difficult people from other cultures and countries?

The world is now a very small place. In the past, an organisation running an office abroad would have seemed glamorous in the extreme but now many organisations have international offices. Staff from overseas offices will spend some time with your company and a lack of communication and understanding could be embarrassing for all.

Not only might your organisation have international offices but it may deal extensively with other nationalities and could possibly have outsourced many of its services to other nations. Years ago, customer service and the manufacturing of your goods would have been considered far too crucial to the front end of business to be passed outside of the organisation, let alone out of the country. However, the international market, increase in technology and the insistence of the customer to drive down costs mean that these two functions alone often operate out of say, China or India. If they are operating from there, you will need staff to liaise and ensure their contract is working effectively.

In addition to these offices or centres overseas, there are also many foreign workers now resident in the UK. Being part of an extending Europe has opened up many possibilities for workers to travel to different countries and fulfil skills gaps. Some come to work in the UK for a very short space of time, and others plan to stay longer, but again you may find yourself working alongside people from different nations, who have had a completely different cultural upbringing, believe in a different set of religious doctrines, and live by an apparently different set of rules.

Economically the UK has, for hundreds of years, encouraged immigration to shore up skills gaps. Not only have those people stayed to raise families and future generations, some have also fully integrated with our society to create a melting pot of culture and history. There should be no need in the workplace to categorise people based on their colour or nationality, but on what they contribute to the business.

The role of diversity in society

As mentioned above, people of different cultures now make up a vast amount of the workforce. To keep pace with the changes in society (and in some instances to promote those changes) specific laws have been put in place that make it illegal to discriminate against anyone in a number of key areas – race and religion being just two of them.

Diversity simply means difference and promoting it acknowledges that so many different people can contribute to life and the working economy. Working with diversity challenges you to consider the benefits of having staff with different backgrounds, cultures and ideas, and to think of the extra value they can bring to the organisation. If you wanted to expand your business overseas you would need specialist advice and perhaps an interpreter to help you set up your business. If you already had employees of that nationality, who are able to help you, the process could be a whole lot easier and you would avoid having to employ consultants and translators.

A word about prejudice. Prejudice is making decisions about people based on little or no factual information. Prejudice is not only illegal, it shows very low levels of thinking ability and emotional intelligence in the individual. To choose not to offer someone an opportunity based on questionable data is nonsense, yet this is what is happening when prejudicial thoughts step in. (Prejudice is covered more fully in the following chapter.)

Exercise

If you are unsure of the key legislation that surrounds equal opportunities and diversity, make sure you attend a training programme every three years at the least, or receive regular updates (there are companies that provide this service). Being caught out will not only cost you a lot of money (the award can be uncapped in some instances, and the liability is a personal one), it can also cost you your job. The bad publicity alone would put you severely out of favour but your organisation may decide to take it further and dismiss you.

Health warning! Note that each country has its own legal system, and equality legislation, for example, will vary. If you have offices abroad or travel you need to research the laws pertaining to that area/state/country.

Stereotypes

When we think of different cultures we often use stereotypes. These are templates that we use to categorise and make assumptions, for example, red-haired people have hot, fiery tempers. If you are reading this book because of some of the difficult people in your life you will know that lots of people have fiery tempers, it is not limited to people with red hair, and so the stereotype is quite unfair. Not only can it be wrong, it can also be very hurtful to the individual. However, stereotypes are not always the 'bad guys' people make them out to be and can have their use – if they are tempered with intelligence and common sense.

Our brains like to categorise and make links and this helps us to short cut thinking processes, enabling us to recognise attributes of objects and people at lightning speed. For example, in Chapter 2 I looked at the brain's capacity to categorise using the attributes of a dog and a lion (because they both have four legs). To take this further, we recognise that a dog is a dog whatever the breed, because although different breeds of dog can look very different, there is some innate 'doggyness' that we identify. Do we differentiate naturally or is it a learnt experience? The nature/nurture debate keeps psychologists up all night and still the clearest answer is that probably it is some of each. When it comes to nurture there is no doubt that our parents and significant elders have had a hand in shaping our stereotypes. For example, when they tell us to keep away from certain types of people, for example, it sets up fears and assumptions that we carry all our lives – except for one fact. All stereotypes can be challenged and when we do challenge them, as with meeting new people, we can find that quite often they fall apart.

Exercise

Do you have a fear or apparently irrational dislike? Perhaps it is for people with beards, moustaches or bald heads? If so, where do you think that has come from? You were not born with this dislike and therefore it must be a learnt response – but where from? Perhaps it was from a fearsome uncle or someone your parents told you to be wary of. Consider this rationally – you know that this fear cannot be true of all people with the same characteristic.

Stereotypes, then, can be useful in grouping ideas together but they are limited in their reality. Put into a cultural context, you may approach someone who looks visibly Asian with one set of stereotyped thoughts and assumptions only to find out that they have very Western ideas and their family have lived in this country for several generations.

Does this mean that we should ignore all stereotypical thoughts then? I would say not. These groupings can be extremely useful in certain circumstances: it is our blind reliance on them that is the problem. Taken delicately as only ever providing a few tentative ideas about the person, they can be most helpful.

To demonstrate how stereotypes can be helpful, let's look at this practically. Your company is opening up an office in Spain and therefore you go to discuss the arrangements with someone called Juan Carlos. You are met by a man who appears typically Spanish, and you decide to greet him with a typical greeting 'Hola. Buenos días?' He seems hughly pleased that you greeted him thus and it augers well for a good working relationship. This worked well because in your brain you assumed that someone with that name, dark colouring, in Spain, coming forward to greet you, just might be Spanish.

Where it does not work well is when you return home and are told that the company is also opening an office in Japan. Later that day you see someone in the corridor who you have not seen before, and he has distinct Eastern looks. You make the assumption that he must be here to discuss the new office in Japan, and so try to greet him with a bow, which he finds hilarious because he is actually the new IT guy from Bexley.

The difference between the two scenarios is the actions and assumptions we make. Our brain does a quick probability test to ascertain the most likely scenario, enabling us to act on it. In the first scenario the probability was high that the man was indeed your Spanish representative. In the second scenario you made the same assumptions but came up with the wrong answer. To make matters worse you are sure that the IT guy will never forget this and you will be laughed at by everyone as he shares his story throughout the company.

Stereotypes and assumptions can be really useful but you need to cross-check the data to make sure it is accurate.

Difficult people or simply different cultures?

Usually when we say someone is being difficult it is because they are not performing in the way we want and expect them to. In many instances people are not actively trying to be difficult, but interpret your words in a different way – in essence 'You say potato and I say patattha'. This leads to a mismatch in understanding. Some cultures operate in a very laid back manner. Asking them to respond quickly is simply not on their radar. They are not being difficult – just different. A credit card company once created an amusing set of adverts that highlighted the differences in cultures across the world. Although the message was that their particular credit card transcended all cultures, it was interesting to see different nuances played out.

It would take a vast knowledge of the world to avoid all these pitfalls, and again you have to be very wary of stereotypes, as there is always an exception to every rule. However, when a problem arises with someone from another culture you have to consider whether it is really a behavioural problem or a cultural one. For example, in some – but not all – Eastern cultures it is considered rude to look someone directly in the eye. In Western culture, eyesight evasion is often portrayed as a sign of sneakiness, someone not to be trusted. Where cultures co-exist you need to be more observant as to whether there is something more than just someone being deliberately difficult.

The other point to consider is that there is a danger that we are always looking for difference. While we are concentrating on difference we are looking at how others are not like us, which can be rather negative. Instead of concentrating on the things that set us apart, how about looking at ways in which we are the same; where there are commonalities. We may be from different cultures but do we both like music, films, eating out, and so forth? When we make friendships we are doing this instinctively. Every friendship we have is made through shared experience – such as finding out we used to live in the same town or were both only children – and therefore finding commonality is far more positive. As a team activity, ask staff to find commonalities. It will be bonding for relationships and you will find that people are not all as completely different as we may suppose.

Effective communication and understanding

If you need to visit or work in another country, you will have to learn the nuances of that country. For example, hand gestures can mean very different things wherever you go. If this is the case, I would recommend that you go on a specialist cultural initiation course so that you do not offend any business contacts or clients. Most people are forgiving to a point but it shows a lack of preparation and understanding to blunder your way in and insult people, no matter what your excuse.

Another alternative is to find a national or expert to guide you gently through any negotiations, and even translate for you. The benefit of this is that they are with you every step of the way and you should never feel out of your depth or alone.

One thing to remember is the five facial expressions we discussed in Chapter 2 that seemingly are international. A smile seems to travel and be understood in any culture and language.

The international team

In terms of business development international teams have the world at their fingertips, and we may be seeing more and more of these around in the future. The world market is huge and trading between countries is the highest it has ever been. In business as in all things there always has been the danger that we only see what is on our own horizon and ignore that beyond. How many of us truly think globally when we consider options for our business? But there are bigger markets out there than we ever dreamed possible. For example the Bollywood film industry far outsells anything Hollywood has to offer. Building diversity into teams can enable more opportunities for tapping into international markets.

If you have people of different cultures in your team and are not capitalising on the benefits of this, then you just might be missing a trick.

If you are already working in a diverse team, or have connections with another team abroad, the very essence of being a member of that team may also be very different. In some cultures the team socialise and lunch together, in others it is strictly business between set hours, and then home. In some Mediterranean countries it is the norm to have longer midday breaks and a late afternoon return to work. This can cause confusion if you are not aware and are trying to contact them between twelve o'clock and two. In the same way that some nationalities greet each other with a kiss, some teams are more intimate with each other than others. Some countries, for example, the UK, are known for their reserve but if you visit teams in other countries don't be surprised to see them acting as if they are family members. If you are not sure, err on the polite but more formal side, and only when someone has you in a bear-hug feel free to reciprocate.

Case study 8

Ravinda Singh has been in the team for five years. She is naturally shy and hesitant in meetings, whereas the rest of the team are quite bullish and forward. Ravinda works with the team's budget and as such does not have the need to communicate regularly with the other team members. She can be quite self-sufficient and that is the way she likes it. Her manager suggested a team day and asked everyone to go. Ravinda was not keen but said she would attend. She was delighted on the day when the main team activity centred around a problem-solving exercise that described being lost in the desert. In the activity was a list of items to be ranked in order for survival. This ranking was then compared in pairs, then in small groups and finally in one large group. The object of the activity was to experience working with consensus as you had to convince others that your order was more sensible. As Ravinda had lived in a hot country she felt very confident in her choice but had trouble getting others to hear her ideas. Every time she wanted to say something, another person cut across her. At one point, even the facilitator could hear her saying, 'I know the right answer here', but no one took any notice.

After the event every member of the team had a meeting with the manager to discuss what came out of the day. Ravinder broke down; she felt that her colleagues had not listened to her advice at all. As her manager, what would you do in this situation and what should you have done on or before the day?

Case study 9

Jay is a Muslim and has been in your team for two years. Her job is to work with older people in the surrounding area, which happens to be a large Muslim community. Jay is fine at her job but you have had some comments from other members of the team that Jay does not try to fit in. They say that she won't go for a drink after work – even a soft drink – and that she seems to want special attention. They have labelled her difficult to get along with and have now told you that she won't be coming to the team day. You are angry because you wanted everyone to be present and, to encourage this, you had booked the conference room over a nearby pub. Is Jay being deliberately difficult? What should you say to Jay?

Case study 10

Peter Farmer is British but has been working with an Italian team for the past three years. Peter is seen as 'our man abroad' and so his company has asked him to take a proposal to Japan and meet the manufacturers there. Peter is not sure what to expect. How could you, as his manager, prepare him?

Conclusion

Working with people of different nationalities can be very interesting. Behind every action and intention there may be a different set of values, rules and thought processes, which in itself is very enlightening and educational.

When looking to work with people of different nationalities take note of stereotypes but do not be led by them. Try to kill as many assumptions as possible and maintain an open mind – even within a different culture there will be further difference and freedom of thought. It might be helpful to remember some generalisations as long as you maintain an open mind to anomalies.

Try to find out as much about people as possible including their practices and religion. This will tell you much about how to behave and what is expected (including dress code). If visiting a team in their own country, try to learn, at the very least, a polite greeting to demonstrate that you have made the effort, and don't forget to smile.

If you are working with a diverse team based in your own country, make sure everyone is up to date on legislation and also knows their rights. Encourage everyone to share information and show active listening. If you think that the presence of someone with a different nationality could be used better by your organisation, speak to the individual first. You will need their help and they won't want to feel exploited or exposed.

INSTANT TIP

Always consider whether any difficulty is in fact cultural before jumping to conclusions and possibly making the situation worse. If in doubt, consult with a cultural expert in your organisation.

09

How do I cope if I am the one being difficult?

Throughout this book we have discussed many types of people and difficult situations and I have mentioned several times about the importance of the dynamic – the fact that between two people there exists a third communication conundrum that appears to work all by itself. My reason for mentioning this again is that, when we look to the possibility of difficult behaviour in others, we also have to look to ourselves. Taking the attitude of problems being 'out there' or always grounded in other people is not sustainable, especially if you seem to be experiencing a whole load of problems with everyone. Have you considered that perhaps the problem is closer to home? If you have never had any management or skills training you may not be dealing with people in the most effective way, and you may have to face up to the fact that it may be your behaviour that is triggering or at least contributing towards the problem.

Remember: I have said this before but it bears being repeated here. You cannot enforce change on other people, you can only change your own behaviour, thoughts and beliefs. You can model the behaviour you want to see in others, and encourage them to follow, but you cannot change them – they have to want to change themselves.

So, if the problem, perhaps, is more to do with you, how would you know? Do you have regular feedback sessions with your managers? Perhaps they have spoken to you or hinted even that your handling of the team or certain situations is not good? Have you had outbursts with staff where they felt able to be honest about your style? Do you seem to be having more problems managing your team than anyone else in the company? Any of these could indicate that you need to reconsider your own style. Ultimately the essence of being a manager is about using your people effectively to achieve the business aims. That can be achieved in a number of ways, but using confrontative tactics, bullying, and aggression will only land you in court. With today's emphasis on transferable skills and a wide job market, staff will only stay as long as they feel content. If you have not had the benefit of any management training, get in touch with the Chartered Management Institute (CMI) and see whether you can attend any courses. It may be that, previously, you have worked for an organisation whose culture rewards and encourages a punitive style of management. Staff are more aware now of working in other ways and therefore you may be managing in a completely inappropriate way for the twenty-first century.

Facing up to your prejudices and assumptions

Now, before we all put our hands up and say, 'Not me', let's get one thing straight – we all hold prejudices and make assumptions. The previous chapter looked at prejudice. The emphasis there was on cultural prejudice but prejudice can take any form and we all have it. Saying that we don't goes against the very fact of how our brains make links and store information (as discussed in Chapter 8). Neural networks are made up of rich connections, and we need to group items to make sense of them. Grouping and labelling makes life easier if you can group people together and treat them all in the same way. For example, 'all dogs have sharp teeth, so you need to be careful when approaching them' is helpful. 'All dogs *will* bite you' is not helpful because it is untrue – some dogs don't bite humans, and the assumption that all dogs will bite will create a life long fear of dogs. So, some prejudices and assumptions are helpful because they enable us to take care, but others produce limitations in our life.

Where do prejudices come from?

Prejudice may be defined as 'where a judgement or decision is made on the basis of little or no factual information' and comes from our life experiences or what we have been told. Notice the emphasis on the lack of factual information. Prejudices are not rational, logical knowledge, they are untested falsehoods that can create serious limitations and blockages to our thinking. Our parents will be responsible for creating some of our deepest prejudices, quite possibly for the best of reasons. Whenever they told you to keep away from certain types of people, to keep you safe, they were setting up prejudice, but before we lay every blame on our parents, we are more than capable of creating or absorbing many others throughout our life, through school and into adulthood. People do form natural groups, such as those based on nationalities, hobbies or physical appearance, and not seeing them as individuals may be extremely limiting. As a manager and employer you may be literally missing a trick by excluding anyone based on prejudiced or outmoded ideas, let alone be acting illegally. Discrimination legislation is there to protect minority groups from this type of treatment and therefore you need to be aware of it and the impact it can make on your business.

Why do we make assumptions?

Assumptions are also part of our short-cutting mechanism. To enable us to make fast decisions, we need to assume certain aspects when the correct data is not to hand. This can be very sensible, for example, all things glowing red are possibly very hot and so we would not naturally reach out and put our hand on a glowing metal plate, just to test it. However, assumptions again can also be very limiting, such as assuming that all mothers of children are not interested in pursuing a career, when in fact as many women with children want to pursue careers as those without children do. In this example, a stereotype (of a classic mother – perhaps modelled on your own mother) has become an assumption (she won't want career progression, she is too busy bringing up her children) and the assumption may form the basis of prejudice if you then decide not to allow this person to go on any courses or to move ahead in her career just because of your opinion of her. Again you are in danger of not acting rationally and seeing the individual as a team member based on their skills, knowledge and ability. Any assumption must always be checked out, as this person may be waiting in the wings to lead your next winning team, but if they are never offered any opportunity, they may leave in disgust (or in an extreme situation, take you to court for discrimination).

Exercise

Think about your staff. What assumptions (or prejudices) may you have been guilty of making without testing out the situation? How does this influence your relationship and interaction with them? Treat everyone as individuals who bring a unique set of talents and abilities to your team, and before you assume that someone may not want to undertake a task or take on some work, check it out with them first.

That critical millisecond called 'choice'

We have already covered the concept that you cannot make anyone change – only make them aware of the problem, model good behaviour, influence and support. Everyone has the choice as to whether to change and that also refers to you. When people tell me, 'I can't help the way I am, I just have a short temper', or 'I don't know why I get so irritated by them, I just can't stop myself', they are ignoring the one thing we have that makes us very different from all other animals on the planet – choice. Animals are behavioural and by this I mean that they do not think 'shall I do this or that?' They react based on instincts and previous behavioural patterns. If you make a sudden movement an animal that feels threatened by this action will react. It will not stop and ask itself whether you intended to threaten it with your action or how their attacking you will make you feel! It is this ability to rationalise and make choices that produces highly intelligent, decision making, rationalising human beings.

You have far more control over your behaviour than you think. There is a critical millisecond called 'choice' where you can think before you act. The same person will tell me that they feel helpless if they shout at a junior member of staff when they make an error, and yet withhold that behaviour if the person who made the error was a senior manager. Since shouting at staff senior to yourself is usually career limiting, they have decided in that critical millisecond to hold their tongue. So they are not really a hostage to their actions all the time, and control is nearer than you may think. We all have much more ability to make a choice as to how we react than we think, but we need to acknowledge it is there for it to be realised.

Don't be a captive to your emotions, don't hide behind 'I can't change' or 'This is who I am' if that behaviour is inappropriate. We can all change, we just need to give ourselves permission to do so and ensure the change is for the better.

Practising positive intent and modelling behaviour

Open any book on self development and the writer will probably advocate the technique of selecting the future position you would like to hold, and then watching the person in that job closely. The method is to learn how people on the next level from yourself behave and even goes as far as to suggest copying their dress sense. The logic behind this technique is to behave so that you will be viewed by others as a potential candidate for the job when a vacancy arises. Now imagine that someone has selected your job as a potential opportunity – what do they see when they watch your behaviour? Are you exhibiting the type of behaviour that really is appropriate for your job?

We are all modelling a set of behaviours that tells the world about us and how we operate, and this can quickly become a blueprint for how the team operates. We are all very good at picking up on body language and verbal interactions, assimilating the information and incorporating it into our own. (Think of how children very quickly learn not only the mannerisms of their parents, but also their weak areas.) Modelling behaviour demonstrates to others what we find acceptable and how we would like to be treated.

The next step on from this is to demonstrate positive intent. This is a term borrowed from the counselling sector and is used to describe how an individual forms a mindset that assumes that, no matter what the other person has said or done, it has been done with positive intent. On the whole, most people are good and do things for the right reasons, even when the results turn out wrong! By blasting off about a failed outcome you run the risk of causing them upset, humiliation and destroying any long-term relationship you may have created. Now, instead of getting angry immediately, assume the mindset that, whatever the outcome, the person was probably acting in the best interests of the team/project at that time. Notice how the situation suddenly becomes different. For a start it is not about them, but about the outcome and possibly, just possibly, it was not actually their fault. We make hundreds of decisions every day – how we will get out of bed, which foot will hit the floor first, tea or coffee for breakfast, to take the train or catch a bus, whether to e-mail someone a birthday greeting or send them a card in the post – and some of them we will get wrong. Everybody makes mistakes a lot of the time but many of the mistakes are not important or go unnoticed. When people make mistakes at work, they assume a higher importance, and some mistakes simply might not be that important, but the tension makes it seem so. By creating a mindset of positive intent we are able to put these mistakes into perspective and react to them on a more authentic, and reasonable, level.

Finding the right immediate response

When someone brings a problem to you, the temptation may be to react emotionally. If that is the right response, then there is time for that later. What we need to do is have an appropriate immediate response that is blame free (after all you don't yet know the facts), and enables you to investigate the situation without destroying everyone in your wake. It is far easier to deal with this rationally at the time, than have to go back and admit you were either wrong or that you acted inappropriately. Another point to note is that if you are considering a future in a large, notable organisation, they are not too happy about putting staff who appear to have no control over their emotions or their behaviour into key jobs. It is too risky as you may bring the company into disrepute as well as into the courts.

The answer is surprisingly easy but may not be your first choice of response, and for this reason it needs practice. The next time someone approaches you with some 'disaster' or mistake, keep calm. Ask them to explain the situation fully, as they see it, and make some notes. At this point, hopefully, the fact that they are talking and you are writing will enable you to keep a reign on any potential outburst. Put all of your remaining energy into active listening rather than speaking. When they have finished, unless very urgent action is required, say something like, 'I need to look into this a little more. Can you come back in half an hour when we can discuss the situation more fully.' If the matter is exceptionally urgent, then try taking three, discreet, deep 'stomach breaths' before replying. This tiny intervention will enable you to insert a break into your normal reaction and immediately give you the choice to take control in a proactive manner, allowing you to reply in a more appropriate way.

Gaining a greater understanding of yourself

Realising that we all have shortcomings is an important part of our adult development, and we can only do this through gaining a greater understanding of our personalities and our motivations. When we face up to certain aspects about ourselves we have the building blocks to move forward and become the people we want to be.

Most psychologists would argue that we are a product of both nature and nurture. In other words, some of our make-up is genetic (and therefore hereditary) while other aspects may be behavioural patterns you have learnt through your life path. You may have inherited your father's nose shape, but is it possible to inherit his temper? Or is it just possible that having a temper tantrum is a learnt response that worked well for your father, and you now adopt as a method to get what you want? I will leave you to decide.

Another complication is that we do not necessarily show our full self to the world. Like the iceberg picture in Figure 9.1, we show and allow others access only to our surface self – the issues we choose to show and a selected part of our personalities. However, there is so much more to us hidden beneath the surface. We may even be denying that this tumultuous block is there, but it contains the history of our lives, our fears and concerns, and makes us the people we are.

Figure 9.1: The iceberg helps us to conceal aspects of our nature from others

Another way to look at this is through the Johari window in Figure 9.2 on page 144.

You can see from this classic model that there is a public arena that is the face we choose to present to the world. It is known to ourselves as well as to others, but take a moment to think about the blind spot and what might lurk there that even you are unaware of. The façade portion represents those hidden secrets that we know about but others don't (such as 'I am not as confident at this as I make out'). You might like to explore what thoughts and feelings are lurking in there. Finally, you can see that there is an area of potential that is known to no one. This represents undiscovered skills and talents that may not have surfaced as yet.

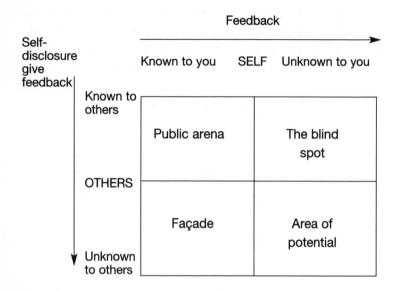

Figure 9.2: The Johari window

You can only give information about what you know and therefore you can provide self feedback on any items in the public arena or façade sections. However, you can get feedback from others to inform the public arena and blind spot sections.

Greater understanding of yourself can start with a thorough understanding of how others see you. Ever done a 360? (And no I don't mean a spin on the spot!) 360 degree feedback is a mechanism whereby the same questionnaire is handed out to:

● those in a role above you
● those junior to your role
● a number of colleagues (both external and internal)

… and of course completed by yourself. (See Figure 9.4 a and b for a sample feedback questionnaire and result sheet.)

This puts you at the very centre of the process and invites everyone around you (see Figure 9.3), hence the term '360 degree', to provide an opinion on your behaviour and competence. This information is then fed back to you via a facilitator.

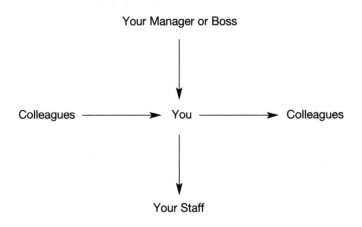

Figure 9.3: 360 degree information on your performance

The resulting information can then be measured statistically against your own opinion of you. 360 degree feedback mechanisms are very powerful when considering your own behaviour and how it impacts on others with whom you work every day. If others view your behaviours and skills lower than you do yourself, you could have a problem whereby you consider yourself far superior to the reality. If you score yourself much lower than others do, it could reveal a serious lack of self-confidence or false modesty. What you are looking for here is an honest summary of your behaviours, and from the feedback you can begin to see how these can be adjusted to work with others more effectively.

In this example we see Chris Smith is being measured against four areas that relate to being able to contribute effectively to, manage and lead, meetings and groups. In this example they are:

EXAMPLE 360 DEGREE FEEDBACK

Questions for Chris Smith, Departmental Manager

In relation to Chris Smith, to what extent would you rate:

1. Level of interaction in meetings

2. Ability to lead groups

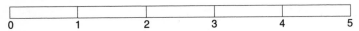

3. Ability to remain focused in meetings

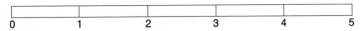

4. Ability to negotiate in meetings

Figure 9.4a: A sample 360 degree feedback questionnaire

EXAMPLE – RESULT SHEET

Results for Chris Smith, Departmental Manager

1. Level of interaction in meetings

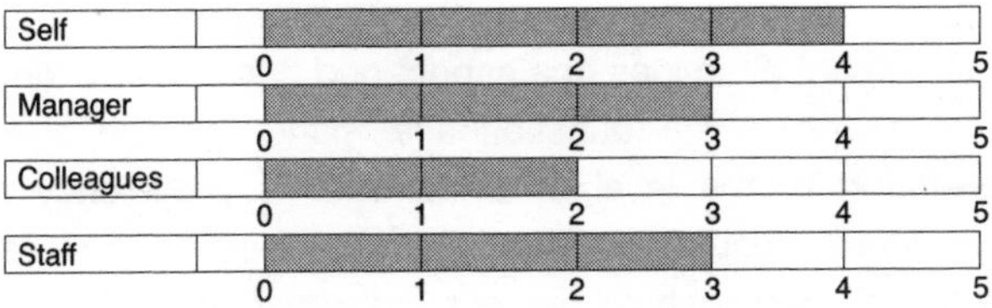

2. Ability to lead groups

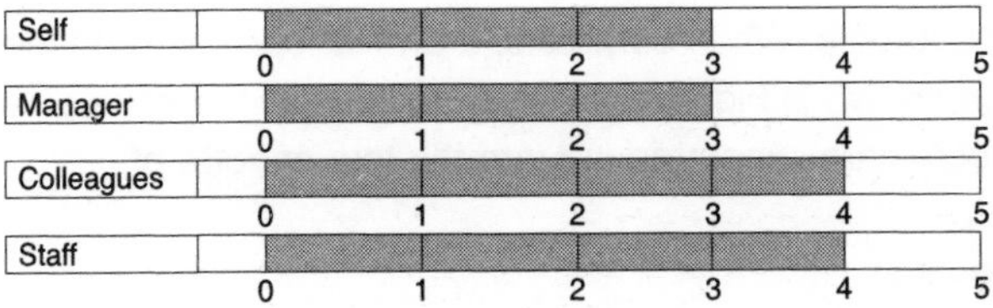

3. Ability to remain focused in meetings

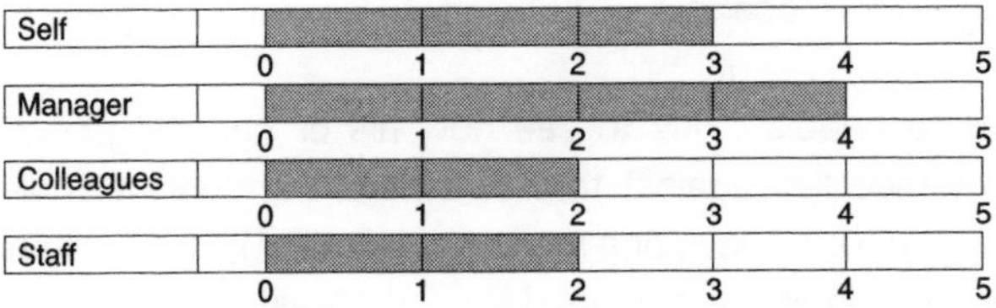

4. Ability to negotiate in meetings

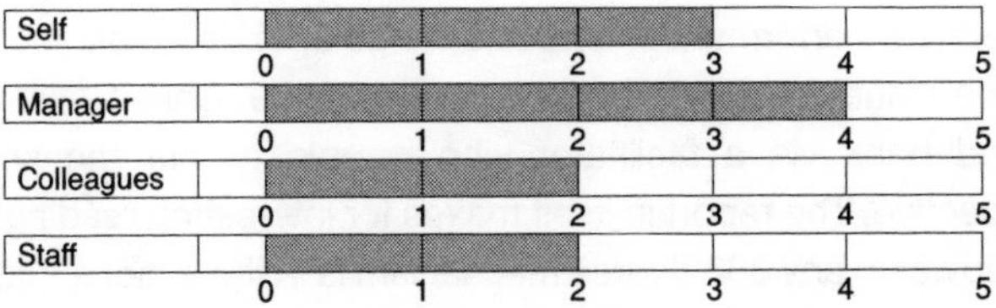

Figure 9.4b: A sample result sheet for the 360 feedback questionnaire

- level of interaction in meetings
- ability to lead groups
- ability to remain focused in meetings
- ability to negotiate in meetings.

Each statement examines one aspect and has a scale from 0 to 5. Each recipient of the questionnaire marks on the sheet their interpretation of the level of Chris Smith's proficiency in each aspect. There is usually an area where the recipient can also enter some text if they wish to present more evidence or explain any aspect of their scoring. All questionnaires are then usually returned anonymously to a data bank where they are all added to Chris Smith's profile. When complete, a profile report is produced (such as that shown in Figure 9.4b) that includes all the scores. Note that the scores are separated out into the four spectra of:

- self
- your manager
- colleagues (usually at your level)
- staff (those that work for you).

This is to enable Chris to see how his or her self perception of performance lies against that of others. Although it is likely that most people only have one manager, there could be multiple entries under 'colleagues' and 'staff'. Usually at least six people are asked to contribute in each of those sections, and the responses are then averaged out. The reason for this is to produce an average view of someone's performance, across a range of skills areas.

The resulting report remains the property of Chris Smith and will be fed back via a facilitator who is able to put the scores in perspective. The report in itself makes for interesting reading but the real power in any 360 degree mechanism is in the actions that follow. You can see in the first example of Figure 9.4b that Chris scores him or herself higher than anyone else. Clearly there is a perception problem here that needs to be addressed. Similarly look, at 3,

Ability to remain focused in meetings. There is a clear discrepancy between Chris's view, the manger's view and everyone else. These areas need looking at in greater detail and they need discussing openly. 360 degree reports need to be shared with your own manager and also with staff. If you are truly interested in your own development as an effective manager you need to be seen to be addressing some of these areas.

When you have your overall report you need to spend some time considering how you feel about the outcome. Do you feel it is a fair representation of you? Is it how you would like to be perceived? Does your style fit with the culture and the way your organisation sees itself in the future? It can be very hard to accept that others find us annoying, a problem or difficult in any way to work with. Defence mechanisms kick in whenever we don't want to hear the message. However, if we do not accept the feedback, then we cannot move forward and make changes. How you accept your feedback will determine your future. If you decide that there is room for improvement then you can work with your direct manager to put forward a plan for development.

Learning and accepting is the key principle – without that you will never fulfil your potential.

Encouraging open communication

If you have engaged in any form of feedback mechanism, whether via 360 degree feedback or simply by using an appraisal system, you have sent a powerful message to those you work with. You are saying openly, 'I am happy to look at myself and work on my performance at work'. This is a very powerful message to send to others as it will encourage them to do likewise, but you are also setting up a precedence for the development work to continue. Once you have started a process such as this there is an expectation that you will be monitoring your performance and making adjustments where necessary – and just possibly asking everyone to measure your skills again in a year's time to ascertain improvement.

Once feedback becomes mutual, it can become part of the culture in your team or group. If you show that you are not afraid of having your own performance at work judged by others, then they will expect the same. This openness will work on a number of levels. Freedom to receive feedback will also enable you to give feedback to others more easily and hopefully build on a feeling of team honesty and maturity, where any problems are discussed openly rather than stored away for some future moment when they can vent forth.

Other ways in which you can be more responsive to other staff are:

- Have an open door policy. If you need to isolate yourself for a particular piece of work that is fine but, in general, make sure everyone knows how accessible you are.
- Use open body language. Make sure your arms use open gestures and move naturally while talking to others (avoid crossing your arms over your chest unless it is natural to do so – it looks defensive even if you don't mean to imply this).
- If you don't have one-to-one meetings with your manager and any staff, re-instate or arrange them immediately.
- Listen to all suggestions and thoughts carefully. Many of the best ideas come from those at the sharp end of the problem.
- Openly acknowledge when someone has a good idea. They will get the credit and you will have the reflected glory of being the messenger. Then look at how, together, you can work the idea up into something more.
- If someone suggests an idea that has been tried before or has no merit, hear them out and then suggest that perhaps they give it some more thought, listing your

concerns. It may be that they decide for themselves not to pursue it, or perhaps they find a way around those areas that have foxed others in the past. Whichever way forward, you are supporting others rather than flattening them.

- Hold meetings where everyone is encouraged to share information and feedback on the group.
- Share your ideas more fully with everyone. Your openness will encourage the same in them.
- Be consistent. Staff will feel more able to approach you if they can be reasonably sure of your reaction.

Case study 11

Gill is a senior administration officer with one member of staff to manage, Sally. She is good at her work tasks but not very good at delegating. Consequently Sally is not really given sufficient work to do. Gill is also a poor communicator. Whenever Sally asks Gill if she can help her out with some work, Gill bites her head off, telling her, 'I can manage!' – even though she clearly can't because the files on Gill's desk are getting higher and higher. Gill is becoming increasingly irritated by Sally, especially as she appears to have finished all her work early each day. She thinks that Sally must be making short cuts to finish so fast, and it is only a matter of time before she catches Sally out. In fact she might even lay a few traps just to see.

The pressures in the situation are obvious to others in the workplace but not to Gill and Sally, as they are too close to the problem and seem to continue regardless.

What is really going on here? Sally wants to help out Gill. She can see her getting overburdened with work and feels that, if she can relieve Gill of some of it, the work would be more evenly distributed. However, Sally is sure that Gill does not trust her for some reason. She cannot think why.

Gill feels intimidated by Sally's efficiency. She recently did the job that Sally does and, even though she has now been promoted, she feels that no one can do the job as well as she did. Further, Gill feels that it is a real cheek of Sally to keep asking her if she needs help – she was promoted to be manager, of course she does not need help! Sally is just trying to show her up. Gill feels that Sally must know that she has a meeting with Jayne, her department head, later that week to discuss her progress as manager.

At the meeting Gill is shocked when Jayne suggests that it is she (and not Sally) who is the problem. That is not how she saw the situation at all, but cannot deny much of the documentary evidence. How can Gill take things forward?

Conclusion

Sometimes the problem is us and there is no escaping that fact, however uncomfortable it may be. There are certain things that we can do to get good feedback on our behaviour and then to implement some changes that will benefit not only the team or staff group, but also challenge some of our ingrained prejudices and assumptions.

Not only should we all be developing and changing in ourselves, but also the world is changing. External factors bring new pressures to dealing with staff. New laws cover different types of discrimination based on changes that have occurred in society. It is easy to get out of date and assume that society has not changed much, whereas in fact the role of the manager is very different from just ten years ago. Help your staff by addressing some of your own demons. It will also demonstrate to them that you are not infallible, and that personal development cuts across all areas of the business.

If you truly are the problem, you will take this problem wherever you go unless you decide to address some of your issues. There are only so many times that you need to be told the same message before you should accept that, if your behaviour is problematic for others, it is also a problem for you too. Moving from job to job will not help the outcome if the root cause moves with it. Listen to feedback from friends and colleagues – just suppose they have a point, what can you do about it? If you have a deep-rooted problem that you need to address, consider therapies such as hypnosis to enable you to change your behaviour. Your career can only benefit from such attentions.

INSTANT TIP

Learning about yourself is to go on a fascinating journey. Question your own motives, challenge your assumptions about yourself and others and consider alternative approaches.

10

How can I manage conflicting team members?

Wherever people are together there is conflict. One person believes that they are not getting the same levels of attention or opportunities as someone else. Another person thinks they are overworked while another thinks they are not trusted. People on their own can be difficult but put them in a team and the web becomes far more intricate because the dynamics create a whole new level of volatility. When you work with difficult people in a team you are not just working with individuals – you are also working with something that is going on between individuals.

Three key things that should under pin all other factors are:

1. You are the manager. It sounds obvious but if you are the team leader or manager you have been put in that place to do just that – manage. Therefore there has to be a point at which you say 'I am going to do something about this', and you have the authority to do so.

2. This is a work situation. We may be able to choose who we marry or live with but we cannot necessarily select who we work with – nor should we. Team workers should be selected for what skills, knowledge and attributes they bring to the team and the work – not the skills, knowledge and attributes you would like in a best friend. Work situations demand that the focus is not necessarily on having fun, it is on achieving goals. People at work do not have to be friends, but they do need to be professional, and are in fact paid to be so.

3. Teams do not need to share everything. If you wish to address an issue with one person, never be tempted to take them to task openly. Everyone deserves respect and should be treated accordingly. Always tackle a behaviour or performance issue in private, away from the rest of the team.

Teams cannot always get along but every member should make an attempt at being professional and this can be noted through their regular one-to-one meetings or appraisals. Being professional is about behaviour, and behaviour can be measured against set targets and monitored regularly. This is not about being heavy handed or a tyrant but it is about noticing what is actually going on in the team and being able to put in preventative measures should you notice things going awry. Should you need additional help, many organisations now either employ or have access to occupational health consultants who are able to come into your working environment and work directly with your team or suggest changes that could be made.

Keeping an eye on the balance

When we select team members we want a good mix of skills, knowledge and attitude, however most recruitment processes look at the two former attributes and perform very little testing on the latter. The consequence of this is that we have teams who should be great performers and cover every angle of a project plan, but actually don't get on or display any attempt at trying.

This is not as unusual as you might think. Consider TV dramas. If the story is always about the incidents themselves they would all have been covered years ago, but they are less about the facts, or the case being investigated – they are more about people. Writers deliberately put two police officers together who don't see eye to eye, or they plunge a doctor who is poor at communication into a situation where communication is the most vital skill. It is within this tension that we see real characters emerge and, let's be honest, when we watch TV dramas we all see living, breathing colleagues reflected in these situations. This is because it actually happens. How many times has the argument been less about the work and more about who sat in someone's chair and – worse – adjusted the settings!

Seemingly petty issues will arise and you will need to keep some semblance of order, if only to ensure the work actually does get done. However, not all teams are full of 'characters', some seemingly exist in perpetual harmony. Is this what we should be aiming for? Not necessarily. Balance is needed in all teams. The danger with too much harmony is that no one is asking the challenging questions. A team of 'Yes' people will still be nodding their approval as they drive off the edge of the cliff!

What you need is a balance of different types of people who have a spread of skills. At this point you may be excused for thinking, 'Well, it's OK if I can select my dream team for balance on all levels, but I inherited my people. They were not chosen so much as handed over.' Actually, this is not as problematic as you may have thought. If it is any consolation, even 'designer' teams have problems because people change. As a result of things happening in our lives none of us are the people we were last week. I may have felt pretty calm yesterday but stressed up to my eyeballs today. Envying a 'designer' team is a hollow emotion. Think about the team you have. If they are problematic, at least you know about it. You know the characters and the more they perform to type the more you can make assumptions about their reactions. When you know where the likely problem areas are, you can begin to create strategies to deal with them.

Now you are seeing the team for what they are, a varied group who have a wide number of talents, albeit in different areas. Their talents need bringing out and acknowledging. Everyone has something to give to the team or an effect upon it. For example, even the quietest person may have a calming effect when there is conflict. Accept that they will have conflicting ideas and upset each other with their different ways of operating. You will need all your higher level skills to work with them – life is nothing if not a challenge – and anyone who does not like people has no business managing teams.

Think also about your own style and balance. You must treat everyone equally. This does not necessarily mean that people should always be handled in the same way, but they must have equal treatment and opportunities. The way in which you handle the team will have far more effect on them than you realise and your balanced approach will help to stabilise the team. Imagine if your parents treated you and your brothers or sisters completely differently, even using a different set of rewards or punishments. You would feel aggrieved and unsettled. You just might kick out about the unfairness of the system and cause more aggravation because of it. This is how team members will react if you do not get your own balancing act right. You might just be guilty of causing some of the terrible situations you think you are working to avoid.

Exercise

Look either at the team you are in or one you are managing. Write down a list of everything that is wrong with the team or any ways you feel the team is not functioning, for example, 'People don't seem to talk to each other.' Now imagine that all these things are positive attributes and the team has been put together for these very reasons. What are the benefits of this behaviour? Using the example given, 'People don't seem to talk to each other' you might decide:

- everyone stays very focused
- perhaps there is not a need for cross-information
- they don't appear to need constant direction
- they are all specialists who benefit from working alone, etc.

Now that these negative comments have been turned into positive comments you will see that the way things are can bring some benefits; you just have not been seeing them.

You may still want to make some changes. However, bear in mind that change is easier to implement if you acknowledge to everyone that there are some positives in what they are currently doing, but that you now need to tweak this to accommodate new ways of working. It is easier for the team to change if they are not told that their behaviour is untenable, poor, difficult, unhelpful – or any of the other negatives you may have used in the past.

Taking a meta or 'helicopter' view

When dealing with people embroiled in difficult situations, one thing becomes very clear. It is very easy to get sucked into the situation. One minute the issue seems to be between two people and the moment you decide to sort it out, you find yourself lost in the detail and taking sides. In fact it is not unheard of for each party to be reconciled in their mutual annoyance at your interference and skip off together into the sunset, leaving you the 'bad guy'.

Several times throughout this book I have mentioned becoming part of the dynamic. When you enter an argument between two people your very presence affects the situation and pastes a third dimension on it. The next time two people are talking together anywhere (yes, even at a party) join them and see how their conversation changes. In the first instance they will at least feel the need to explain what they were discussing and then, depending on you, they may even modify their language to suit their new audience. It is particularly interesting to see the changes in two people in discussion at work who are suddenly joined by their manager. However, not all effects on the dynamic are unhelpful. The sudden presence of a manager, for example, can curtail bad language and prevent a petty argument becoming an offensive onslaught from which it is difficult to recover.

It is impossible not to interject to sort out a problem situation, that is after all part of your role, but because of the dynamic it is important to try to limit your effect on the other team members, other than in a positive way. So how can you do this?

In the first instance, when there is a problem in the team that concerns only two people, aim to isolate them from the team while you try to mediate. As I described above, others will get sucked into the argument and start taking sides, so ask the people concerned to move with you to your office or a private room, rather than trying to deal with the situation in the full glare of everyone. (Quite often the mere physical movement from their desk space to another room will effect a change in behaviour.)

When there ask each person, without any interruptions, to state their situation – first one and then the other. Do not interrupt yourself other than to clarify any details, and make notes if you feel this would be helpful. At this point, there just may be a way forward if the issue is fairly simplistic but the likelihood is that the problem centres around either lack of communication or consideration. If this is the case, you need (without getting involved yourself) to be able to take on a 'helicopter' view to see what is actually going on. Many adult-to-adult situations are actually very similar to childhood situations that have played out over the years. Imagine two children in the playground are having a disagreement. You can see what is actually happening, where the trigger points are, how one is antagonising the other – and it is played out as graphically as on a television screen. Although the people in front of you are older, they are still playing out these games with each other and it helps the situation to explain this in such a way that they can see for themselves what is going on. This technique is often called the meta position and it requires each person to imagine that in their disagreement there are not just two positions (each other), there is a third position – the meta position (see Figure 10.1).

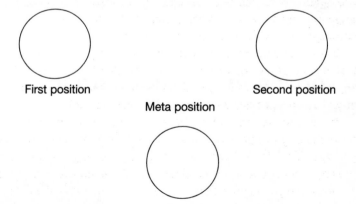

First position   Second position

Meta position

Figure 10.1: The meta position

The meta position is like a spirit – or someone in a helicopter – hovering over the situation and seeing what is really going on. It is similar to when you watch a TV soap: you, the watcher, can see what is going on between the characters' argument because you are separated from any shared emotion. The characters cannot see it because they are blinded by their own emotions, and we watch with bated breath as they stumble on and make one bad decision after another.

To use this technique, ask each person individually, when they take up this position, about what they see. What is actually happening? Where were the crunch points? Is this disagreement really about the situation as presented or is there some other smouldering situation going on? Do not be surprised if one of them laughs because the situation suddenly appears childish, or mentions that it all appears so silly. Do not be drawn into comparisons yourself and, as soon as you can, move on to how this either could have been prevented, and/or how the situation can be solved (draw on that meta or helicopter position again to see how they would solve it if they were watching it from above).

This is a powerful technique that is used in resolving many disputes and will enable everyone to identify trigger behaviours that can prevent a recurrence of the situation in the future. It also prevents you from being sucked into the argument, as you are able to stay impartial and guide the process.

Divorcing the situation from the emotion

In every altercation there will be a great deal of emotion. Emotion is great at helping us to express our hurt to other parties and it also helps us to free ourselves from pent-up frustrations that would make us ill were we to internalise them. Emotion, then, has very useful functions, but it is not effective when it clouds thinking processes and prevents rational decision making. Telling someone in distress, 'Don't be so emotional', is not very helpful either at the time or in the long term.

Dealing with emotions in the team needs a gentle touch. There is no point, as mentioned above, in expecting an emotional person to act rationally so shelve any solid actions for now. Let's deal instead with the emotions and try to get those under control. When people are upset it is understandable that they may want to cry. This can be a really useful way of dealing with emotion. Take them to an area of privacy and allow them to cry for as long as they need to, offering only a tissue and firm support. Do not try to elicit details from them or try to engage in a conversation. No one cries for ever, and they will eventually cry themselves out. Crying is the body's natural reaction to shock, upset, anxiety and so forth, so don't berate them for it, but offer encouraging speech such as, 'Crying is cleansing and I think you needed to get that emotion out.'

If the emotion is anger then again try to steer them to an area away from other people in case they say something that they later regret, or try to draw others in. Do not mention the outburst, instead suggest that they take some deep breaths to help gain a sense of control and equilibrium. Acknowledge their anger, 'I understand you feel angry about all of this', but add a way forward, 'so I think a five-minute break might be helpful before we continue this conversation.' This statement has the added, but subtly understated, proviso that you will not be conversing until they calm down. As I have mentioned before, anger is a frightening emotion but it is not long lived. No one can stay in a state of anger for ever as it is immensely tiring, therefore your staff member will calm down, and you will then need to work with whatever behaviours remain (despair, sarcasm, a willingness to listen, and so forth).

Once you have dealt with the emotion, the resulting behaviour returns to behavioural management as detailed in Chapter 1. Poor behaviour can be managed through your organisational policies on behaviour. The main aspect is to ensure the communication continues. You will never resolve a situation if the communication stops.

Identifying core team objectives

One way of minimising the possibility of team discord is to set some core team objectives. Obviously this works well when everyone is working largely to a similar outcome, but it can also be helpful when people are doing very different tasks. It gives such people focus and a sense of being in a team when perhaps they had felt more like a specialist and a lone worker.

Whenever you set your team their objectives, whether this be at appraisal or any other time, the emphasis is often on creating individual objectives for each person. Objective setting does not have to be done this way. Several objectives can be set at team level and these are the objectives that everyone in the team shares responsibility for. This does not mean that everyone is doing the same thing. Although the objective is the same, the way in which each member fulfils it does not have to be. For example, you may decide that one of your core objectives for the team is:

To resolve every query put to the team within 48 hours.

For Mary this may be handling responses on the e-mail system, for John it is the phone enquiries and for Sarah it is the postal responses. While these are all from external sources Jim may handle the internal queries from other departments. All the team are achieving the same objective but by different methods and it is this striving for a common objective that bonds the team and gives them a common purpose.

All team objectives should be written in unambiguous language and very often the SMART mnemonic is used to ensure this is so. SMART stands for:

S – specific – make sure the objective is specific

M – measurable – the objective will need to be measured to ensure it can be monitored

A – agreed/achievable – it must be agreed with your manager and achievable in context

R – reasonable – it must be within your job remit and possible

T – time-based – it must have a time limit attached to it.

Setting your objectives by this criteria usually ensures they are all-encompassing and will face up to scrutiny later on, should there be any disagreement.

Not all objectives need to be team ones. As part of appraisal you may have three objectives across the team and then each team member may have another three – or more – pertaining to themselves.

The last point about team objectives is that they should be written down in some way (to provide credibility) and may even be made into aspirational posters or form the basis of a customer charter for the team.

Exercise

If you had to select three team objectives for your team, what would they be? Now rewrite them in SMART format so that they can easily be measured and consider whether introducing team objectives would have a beneficial effect on your team.

Reinforcing the benefits of a positive outcome

Teams are always on the flux. If they are working well as a team then any upset from one team member will affect everyone as there should be some group empathy taking place. That people should care for each other is natural. So there will always be ups and downs and imagining, therefore, that there is a team Nirvana out there is very unlikely to be realistic. However, you do need to have a big picture of how you would like the team to be. If you are to work together, for the good of the company, you need a vision. That vision is likely to see all your team enjoying the benefits of a healthy team support system. Anticipate that the team will have problems from time to time, but feel confident there is a range of solutions available to enable disputes to be reconciled and the team to be supported through their more difficult times.

Your view of the team may sound very obvious to you but unless you communicate it to the rest of the team, how will they know? You have been provided with a range of techniques throughout this book and your organisation will have policies in place to resolve situations between staff. However, none of them will be any good unless you are aware of them, use them and make the team aware of them also. Throughout all difficult situations and when dealing with difficult team members always stress your belief in a positive outcome. This will give everyone faith and hope that, whatever the problem, it can be resolved effectively, and the team can move forwards.

One final point to note is that, when you work through difficulties, it can make you much stronger. You will learn more about your team (and yourself) this way than by sailing through untroubled waters.

Case study 12

Donna has been working for J. Salmon Ltd for four years. It is a small company and everyone does very different jobs. Donna deals with customer sales and is very clear about her role. She knows when to hand her work over to the next person and, because she has always operated like this, she does not see the need to change. John Salmon has brought in a new team leader because he wants to expand the business. All the staff have been told is that Andy Fry has joined and will be trying to move the business forward. Andy has come from a background of strong teamwork and believes he is the right man to pull them together and instil a sense of 'teamliness'. Donna is not impressed and rejects everything Andy has tried to put in place. She does her work but is surly and now cuts herself off from everyone, only speaking when she has to. Andy knows he needs to do something with Donna – but what?

Case study 13

Jane Day works in a large insurance company. The company moved to flexible working some months ago but mostly people sit in the same place they always have done. Jane sits on the right side of the main team area. Sandra Lucas has been on maternity leave for a year and has just returned. While she was away Jane acted up into her position (a promotion) and sat where Sandra did, at the front of the team. Following her maternity leave, Sandra asked to come back for two days a week and this has been accepted with Jane continuing in the acted up position. Sandra has only been back for a month but when she comes in she sits in her 'old' position, thereby forcing Jane to sit in her original seat. The seating arrangements should not matter because of the flexible working arrangement, but Jane is furious and has started picking on Sandra. This has now reached a head and an argument is in the air. What would you do?

Case study 14

David Cannon has worked within the same team for several years and most people would agree that he is very good with computers. In fact, he sees himself as a bit of an expert although that is not the focus of his job. Two months ago Lucas Albright joined the team and he is excellent at IT. He even suggests that the team create and maintain a website and move a lot of their work online. He has suggested giving lessons to anyone who is unsure and wants everyone to upskill as much as possible. He is young and enthusiastic and seems to suggest that IT is for everyone, pushing David's nose firmly out of joint. David is now sulking and withdrawn, having very little to do with the team. Lucas finds this behaviour amazing and cannot fathom it. He uses David's silence as approbation for pushing his own ideas further forward – after all, if David says nothing then he can just push ahead, can't he?

Conclusion

Both working in and managing teams can be very rewarding, however always anticipate that at some point some behaviour will need addressing – and ensure that you can handle it. This awareness of human nature together with a strong positive vision will set you in good store. It is only by being an exceptional communicator yourself that you can handle team dynamics. Very often the outward manifestation of the problem is not the actual cause at all and that, together with volatile and uncommunicative behaviour, makes it difficult to see inside many problems. However, you can only deal with the presenting behaviour until someone explains the detail, and then you need to be aware of the emotional fall out.

Emotions are a natural reaction to many situations so if that is an area where you feel you may come unstuck, find a training course that deals with this so that you feel confident with your own reaction. There are many training courses (or independent facilitators) that will help you (and the team) work through major issues. Help is never far away and as you grow in skills, you will grow in confidence.

INSTANT TIP

You are aiming for an honest and open team that feels able to manage their own problems within a framework of safety and trust. When you deal with a problem stay calm, be supportive and in control. Always focus on positive outcomes by keeping one eye on the rainbow.

Your Twelve-Point Tool Box

During this book you have considered a number of case studies. In real life, situations vary considerably, however, in this chapter I have proposed a number of solutions and aspects you need to consider.

To begin with you may like to think through some general techniques that can help you deal with many difficult situations, a Twelve-Point Tool Box of ideas and techniques that have been discussed and demonstrated throughout this book:

1. **Don't take it personally or get personal.** Anger or emotion will flow but it is rarely about you personally, it is about the situation. Never allow the altercation to become personal on either side as it makes discussions to find a solution almost impossible.

2. **Plan for emotion, it is only natural.** People seem terrified of emotion but it is only natural, up to a point. Never accept any form of violence. If you feel uneasy about how to handle the general emotions of others (crying, sadness, despondency and so forth), have a

strategy in place for each. Expect emotions rather than
see them as something of a surprise, then you are ready
to deal with them more effectively.

3. **Listen, acknowledge, validate.** What the other person
is saying is important. Exercise active listening.
Acknowledge their concerns (although never accept
blame at this stage). Validate their feelings. Use speech
such as, 'If this is what has happened I can see how it
would have made you upset. Let me look into this and
then we can speak again.'

4. **Be calm and assertive.** If you all become excited by
emotions you will not be thinking straight. Stay as calm as
you can and model supportive body language. Don't be
afraid to be assertive, you are the manager after all. If the
conversation seems to be going around and around, or is
no longer productive, someone needs to curtail it, and
that someone is you. Don't ask, tell. Say something like,
'I have noted down the main points and I really need to
look into this now. Let's meet to discuss this again later
today/tomorrow.'

5. **Putting the onus on yourself.** Quite often many difficult
people are bound up in themselves and their own feelings.
To change focus or take the heat out of them, put the
onus on yourself. Saying something such as, 'Let's check
that I've been clear.' Suddenly, this makes the
conversation about you, and that makes it more easy to
control.

6. **Leave them the bus fare home.** Allow others either to
withdraw their comments, apologise or change their
minds with their dignity intact. It helps no one to crush
people, show them up in front of others or expose them to
ridicule. That will only cause long-term bad feeling from
which you may never recover.

7. **Make a break – changing body language.** When things get very heated, the mind and the body work together and get locked. When people are angry you often see them rooted to the spot or, if they are upset, they may glue themselves into a chair. In essence, to maintain concentration on their feelings, people often get stuck in one physical position. Get them to change that position and it can change the way they think. Ask them to come with you to another room or move over to another chair. It can 'unstick' their thinking.

8. **Take ten.** If things become very heated or overly emotional, call for a break. Get a coffee, take a walk and return to the situation anew. It is amazing how different things seem after a ten-minute break.

9. **Own your feelings.** When speaking use first person language such as, 'I think' or 'This is how it affects me'. It is much more powerful than 'people think' or 'I've heard on the grapevine that you ...', which cannot be proven or justified.

10. **Levelling technique.** The power ratio in dealing with difficult situations can easily be unfairly balanced, with the manager holding most of the cards. Unless you want to rule by fear you need to level out this balance of power. Start by encouraging mutual feedback and open discussion and if you have handled a situation particularly well, be open to accepting feedback on your own performance.

11. **Know the 'rules' in your company.** Every company has its own policies, rules and culture. Learn them and abide by them, otherwise you could find a difficult situation with someone else rebounding on you. A manager is judged not only on their own performance but also on how they interact and get the best out of others. Get it wrong and you could find yourself out of the door instead of the protagonist.

12. **Stay positive.** You have lived and worked with people all your life and that is great grounding for dealing with any difficult situation. You will not be able to solve everything for everyone but you need to be able to look in the mirror every night and know you handled things in the best way that you could.

Case Study Suggestions

Case study 1

(See page 70.)

In the first instance Bob needs to try to speak with Pete. He may have to start by suggesting that they have regular one-to-one meetings and mention that they were so helpful to iron out any problems when he worked with Phil. If he can get Pete to agree to this, he can then put 'New information' on the agenda and start to work from there, tackling each problem in turn. If Pete refuses to have the one-to-one meetings, Bob may need to speak to a senior manager about the situation. As Pete is working on a project there must be a project owner who would have a vested interest in Bob's situation. In the meantime, though, Bob could also approach his old manager, Phil, about some mentoring.

When it comes to shouting at the team, you all need to meet to discuss whether this is appropriate behaviour or not, given the situation and circumstances, and then take action as a group to face Pete with his behaviour. Bullying and harassment is illegal and should not have to be tolerated.

Case study 2

(See page 71.)

As a starting part Poona needs to speak with HR or personnel. They can advise her on her specific situation and support her in her decision. Poona has two options: she can leave, but will probably always feel that she ran away from the situation, or she can stay and fight. If she decides to stay, the law is on her side and she should never have to put up with racist comments. Racial discrimination cases are well supported through the court system and, therefore, although it may be traumatic to work through the process at the time, she would at least feel that she has stood up for her rights. This will be a difficult decision for Poona to make, but you can assure her that you will support her all the way (and you might also tell her that not all managers are like that).

Case study 3

(See page 85.)

In the first instance Colin needs to speak confidentially with his manager. Simon's remarks are completely out of order and the comments regarding his dancing are nothing to do with work – that could be considered harassment and so Simon needs to be warned through the correct channels. The fact that Simon views their work in such a competitive way indicates that he is probably not a good team player. He obviously feels unsettled by Colin or inferior in some way, otherwise he would not feel that he needed to 'win'.

Colin needs to speak to someone about this situation so that he not only has a support mechanism but also a number of coping strategies. Sometimes the coping strategy is avoidance so perhaps Colin could work from home and come into contact with Simon as little as possible. It is not ideal although it would keep them working together on the project – but apart.

(Simon also needs careful and effective feedback about his behaviour. It is not acceptable to treat others in this way and joking is no excuse for poor behaviour. He needs to be given strict targets for changing his behaviour. If left unchecked there is a danger that Simon will turn into a bullying manager.)

Case study 4

(See page 104.)

The issue here, then, is two-fold:

1. Why does Peter Smith keep returning items?
2. This takes up too much of your time.

In the first instance you will need to do a thorough investigation as to the nature of the faults. Every business has an amount of faulty merchandise, but how is it that more than the usual percentage has found its way to Peter Smith? If you feel the situation is more about Peter Smith than the products, you need to decide whether to:

● face him with the issue, risking the fact that he may feel exposed and not come back – but hey! you don't need people like him and you are one hour better off every week!
● ignore it as just the way he is and look around for another person to deal with him.

However, there is another option. If you feel that Peter Smith's complaints are valid and he is a valued customer, you may consider involving him more in the business. Rather than trying to bat him off, ask him to come in to meet you and explain how he sees the situation – you must be doing lots of things right for him to keep returning. Explain how valued a customer he is (he may just be looking for attention) and involve him in a way of fast-tracking his concerns. After all, if you can save time and he feels he has helped implement a process that he benefits from in the long run, then you are both winners.

Case study 5

(See page 104.)

Firstly, you need some facts and figures. How many people have complained? When did this start to happen? What is the impact on the business?

The next step is to speak with Patsy's manager. It may be that they are unaware of the situation and the problems it is causing, but leave them to speak to Patsy and find out any more information. Ask to meet with them again a week later. If there is either no improvement, an outcome of 'that's just the way we work here', or an unsatisfactory answer, suggest that all the key managers in the critical chain of customer service meet to problem-solve the situation. Keep all blame out of the discussions and use a system of business process mapping to measure the time taken to undertake each process, then use the meeting to design a more streamlined process. By keeping the discussions away from blaming any one department, and by taking a joint problem-solving approach, you may even find ways of speeding up your own processes.

Although success is not guaranteed people are much more likely to be helpful if they understand the full implication of the delays.

Case study 6

(See page 118.)

In the first instance I would look at the new contract and ask myself whether there are any statements that actually cause me unease or is it that I have never seen them stipulated in such a way before. Also, is there anything that I actually disagree with. Then I would ask to meet with Mark again to discuss the finer points. (Going to his father would only irritate Mark and if Mr Faulkner really is retiring, he is unlikely to be interested.) Remember, everything is always up for negotiation if you can keep your head. You may want to consider that Mark may just be over-eager. Taking over a good business is an exciting prospect and he may not have had much real experience to date. It might be worth pricing up some of Mark's competition before the meeting and also mention your long-term relationship with the company. Keep the conversation open and don't burn any boats. It could be that Mark has much to learn and losing business can be a salutary lesson. If you part company, keep the door open – you may still do business with them in the future.

Case study 7

(See page 119.)

Screws and bolts are not that difficult to source from other places but the point here is that you lost control and let the problems with Leonard Smith blow out of proportion. Perhaps, until this moment, Leonard Smith had been a better than average supplier who just happened to slip up twice – and, because you did not do the analysis, you made a snap decision.

You have several options. You could go back to Leonard Smith or source a new supplier but this would require you to come clean to your boss who will want to know why you are reverting or changing supplier again. The likelihood of the truth coming out is quite high. Your other alternative is to meet with Putnams to see whether they can improve their record of service or their price. If they seem keen to engage you will know that they value your custom but, if not, it is clear that you are just another customer who is going to have to keep waiting and paying. Only you can decide what you would do in this situation, but the most important lesson to be learnt is that you need to react with more precision and less emotion in future.

Case study 8

(See page 131.)

It is clear that Ravinda found it difficult to be heard on the day and felt shunned by her colleagues. Ravinda works on her own, is quiet and rarely has to interact with the rest of the team. Even if she does have to speak to everyone it is on a one-to-one basis. She probably found the whole team experience quite difficult and fairly intimidating. Had you thought this through prior to the exercise you could have introduced a number of rules, whatever would be appropriate for your team. You could have:

- made a list of team ground rules (including respecting the views of others and allowing everyone to speak)
- used a method for speaking, e.g. only the person holding the ball (or baton) can speak
- kept the groups much smaller all the way through the exercise
- told every team that there may be experts among them – but they have to look out for them

and so forth.

Case study 9

(See page 132.)

In the first instance you need to speak to Jay to find out what her problem actually is. It seems as through the situation has got out of hand and you need to find out whether her refusal is cultural or wilful. It is fairly well known that drinking alcohol is forbidden within the Muslim religion but what is not always so well known is that Muslims should not be in places where alcohol is present, for example a bar or club. You need to ask Jay if this is the problem and if the team day were to be set in an alcohol-free environment, would she then attend.

Case study 10

(See page 133.)

Just because Peter has been working in one country does not mean he could be sent to another one and understand the culture. However, it is true that travel broadens the mind, and he may be more attuned to changes in culture than his less-travelled colleagues.

It is unlikely that his experiences in the previous country will be of much relevance in Japan and he will need a cultural initiation course so that he does not offend anyone and understands how to dress and interact. He will also need a way of translating language and written text so that he is not only able to negotiate on behalf of your company but also find his way around.

Case study 11

(See page 151.)

Being faced with the fact that you are the problem or at least part of it can be a real shock. Firstly Gill needs to get over that shock and take on board some honest feedback. If she is not able to do this, Jayne will have to move straight into setting Gill targets for her behaviour and monitoring her more closely. If Gill can accept this, Jayne can work with her to see where her fear of delegating comes from and how it could be improved. Gill would probably also benefit from mentoring as she is new in post.

Gill also seems to be a poor communicator and Jayne would need to find out where Gill has specific problems and whether there is an internal course or some coaching that would enable her to improve.

Case study 12

(See page 167.)

Andy needs to take a firm stance with Donna. He has already tried the soft approach but she is wilfully continuing. He therefore needs to explore his organisation's policies on conduct, while informing Donna that this is what he is doing. Donna needs to learn that she is paid to do a job in a certain manner and that if she is refusing this, then she and the job may need to part company. Andy must also be careful to log all details of Donna's behaviour, including times and dates, in case she refutes his claim.

Resources

Books

Bird, P. (2008) *Time Management* (Instant Manager), Hodder Education

Covey, Stephen R. (1999) *The Seven Habits of Highly Successful People*, London: Simon & Schuster

Konstant, T. (2008) *Overcoming Information Overload* (Instant Manager), Hodder Education

McDermott, I. and O'Connor, J. (1997) *Practical NLP for Managers*, Aldershot: Gower Publishing

Mannering, K. (2006) *Thrive and Survive the Nine to Five*, Bank House Books

Ribbens, G. and Thompson, D. (2000) *Body Language* (Instant Manager), Hodder Education

Shapiro, M. (2007) *NLP* (Instant Manager), Hodder Education

Somers, M. (2008) *Coaching* (Instant Manager), Hodder Education

Contacts and websites

Karen Mannering: karenmannering.co.uk
Karen Mannering: dealingwithdifficultpeople.co.uk
Mo Shapiro: moshapiro.com
Jane Chapman: jane@positivesteps.co.uk
Peter Cook: humandynamics.demon.co.uk

Index